ONCE UPON
— A PEW —

*More fun than
having the preacher over!*

A collection of true, funny things
that have happened in church…
numerous quips, pulpit bloopers,
typos, and biblical backfires.

by
Ken Alley, P.K.

ONCE UPON A PEW

***More fun than
having the preacher over!***

A collection of true, funny things
that have happened in church…
numerous quips, pulpit bloopers,
typos, and biblical backfires.

by
Ken Alley, P.K.

PARTNERSHIP BOOK SERVICES
Hillsboro, KS 1995

As far as the copyright of this book is concerned, all other media are welcome to use individual excerpts without seeking permission, as long as credit is given to: *Once Upon A Pew.*

For discount schedule contact Partnership Book Services, 135 North Main, Hillsboro, KS 67063
1-800-442-1670
FAX 316-442-7454

© Copyright 1995
GOOD IDEA PUBLICATIONS
Ken Alley, President
P.O. Box 552
York, Nebraska 68467

Second Printing 1996
Library of Congress Catalog Number: 95-069412

ISBN: 09645085-0-8

Publisher's Cataloging in Publication
(Prepared by Quality Books Inc.)

Alley, Ken.
    Once upon a pew / by Ken Alley.
    p. cm.
    Preassigned LCCN: 95-69412.
    ISBN 0-9645085-0-8

    1. Religion--Humor.   I. Title.

PN6231.R4A55 1995   818'.02
                                     QBI95-20428

Dedicated to my wife Mary,
and my kiddos, Deeda, Joey K. and Bri.

Thanks to Sara Dinkelman, Karen Palik, and Mary Tieken for finding close to a zillion typos. To Vaughn and Judi Domeier, John and Bettye Jo Hamm, and Mike and Sharon Westerfield for their enlightening opinions. Thanks to Mike Anderson for the catchy title.

A merry heart doeth good like medicine.

— *Proverbs 17:22*

ONCE UPON A PEW
By *Ken Alley PK*

CHAPTER

1) Things Preachers Do and Say 1

2) Out of the Mouths of Kiddos. 25

3) Out of the Mouths of Typewriters 61

4) Miscellaneous Bloopers 95

5) Wedding and Marriage Oops. 139

6) Things Pondered During a Dry Sermon . . 145

7) Contributions from "Life, Humor, and Biblical Briefs," the "Lutheran Witness" Magazine, and the "Lutheran" Magazine . 157

8) Dear PK 183

9) Associated Hymns 197

10) Sunday Mornin' Shame 205

INTRODUCTION

The first time this church humor idea struck me, I was driving home from a convention. My mind wandered to my family, then to my childhood. Dad was a preacher, making me the dreaded P.K. (Preacher's Kid).

Church services were a big part of my up-bringing. There are many preachers in my family, but I never got the calling. I was to serve mankind as a chiropractor.

I started reminiscing about when I was five or six and squirming through another sermon. I looked forward and saw a two-year-old girl standing on her seat. She grabbed the back of the pew ahead of her, leaned way forward and tumbled head over heels into the next pew. I laughed so loud, there was no doubt Mom would be taking me out for a licking, but it was worth it! It was the funniest thing I had ever seen in my young life: whatever punishment was OK.

These memories caused me to laugh uncontrollably. I wondered if there were others who had had similar experiences in church, just good hilarious happenings that cracked you up. Maybe I'd start collecting them. It would make fun conversation, if nothing else.

Back to work, kids in school, pay the bills, etc., and a couple of years went by. It wasn't until my family and I were sitting in church one Sunday and towards the end of the sermon the preacher remarked, "We should all strive daily to be better Christians...for

Christ's sake!" It was almost like he was swearing. (I know what he meant, but maybe he should have ended that sentence with "…for the sake of Christ" instead).

My wife and I looked at each other and chuckled hard inside. I hate getting tickled in church; it's rude.

The idea had surfaced again so I decided to attack my "Blooper" project full blast. I worked on an ad that I was going to run in a couple of national church magazines. It read like this:

PULPIT BLooPERS

Sooner or later it happens! You didn't mean to say it that way, but you did, a biblical backfire! Send us your (or someone else's) humorous goofs, slips of the tongue, or any funny occurrence that happened during a church service. Names won't be used to protect the embarrassed. Please respond quickly, we are on a deadline. Upcoming book proceeds will go for Christian education. Send to Ken Alley, P.O. Box 552, York, Nebr. 68467

My "respond quickly" was a brainstorm I invented to get people to send me their stories fast…it didn't work. I learned I had to drag stories out of people, even from friends at my own church who knew I was writing this book. In some instances, it was as if they thought nothing about church should be funny.

My "Christian education" promise was so God would be on my side in this venture. I didn't think it would hurt. My intentions might have been in a gray area because I was actually thinking of the royalty checks putting my kids through a Christian college.

After my ads appeared, I started receiving humorous stories. The first thing that usually came to mind every morning was, "I wonder what will be in the mail this morning." Hearing from people all over the nation has sparked me out of bed for quite a while now. Many remarked what a good idea I had and wished my book well. Several preached sermons about how church should be fun and not a drab experience as seen on so many worshippers' faces. I have to agree.

It was tons of fun when I would mention my book to patients at my office. Invariably, some would say, "You know, I remember once when I was at church and..." They would go on and on telling me about their experience. Sometimes it became disruptive because they would get so tickled at their encounter with church humor that they couldn't finish their story. I would have to wait for them to calm down and regain their composure. Sometimes I would go see another patient, but when I returned the giggles would start all over again.

It took four years to accumulate this material. As soon as I thought I had heard the last story, someone at the coffee shop or the Community Center would corner me and ask, "Aren't you the preacher that's writing the church joke book?" I would tell them no, I am a chiropractor who is writing a book about true, funny things that happen in church.

Then he would say, "Well, yeah, that's what I meant," and he would proceed to tell me his story. Sometimes I couldn't see what was so funny until the next day, but most stories proved valuable.

One day I was having a great lunch at my mother-in-law, Edna's. She said, "You know Kenny, I remember when Mary (my wife, her daughter) was three years old and we were in mass. After the choir was through singing, she stood up on the pew, threw her arms open like she did at home in front of the mirror and sang out loud, "Let Me Go Lover!"

I told her that was cute and I'd use it in my book. What I felt like saying was: "EDNA, YOU KNOW I'VE BEEN COLLECTING THESE STORIES FOR SEVERAL YEARS AND NOW, OUT OF THE BLUE, YOU COME UP WITH THIS GREAT ONE!!" I decided I would get a lot more out of her lunches without giving her the third degree, so I let it go. It makes me wonder how many great stories there are out there. We don't need to make up jokes, life is funny just the way it is.

For you zealots who think this book is improper and blasphemous, lighten up! God has a sense of humor, he made you didn't he?

A very good man, Dr. Alan J. Ashley told me time and again:

ENJOY!

"Humor provides a strong bond that draws a people together, establishes a sense of belonging and promotes a particular culture. Humor which grows out of our religious nature is very important in developing our concept of who we are. Humor does unify us in many ways. Not only does Dr. Alley's book provide us with a humorous look at who we are, but he provides us with a really 'good laugh' for those days we need a lighthearted look at life."

— Dr. Mike Westerfield PHD
York Christian College, York, NE

"This is the funniest book I've ever read!"

Millions and millions of people have said this, and I can prove it because I have all their names at my office…somewhere.
— KA

— Warning —

Do Not Read This Book
During Church Services!!!!

Chapter 1

Things That Preachers Do and Say

Time after time a well-meaning preacher would pray publicly, "Lord, be with those who are sick of us." Finally someone took him aside and suggested that he pray, "Be with those who are sick among us."
— *Marvin Greene, KS*

Speaking on communication between husbands and wives, the preacher said, "Husbands come home at the end of the day and want peace and quiet, while the wife needs to talk with him. All she's heard all day is "ga ga, doo, doo." (instead of da, da, goo, goo.) He stopped, looked startled, realized his mistake and said "Oh well, they say that too."
— *Bettye Alley, TN*

A lawyer-preacher leading a prayer before the sermon, made routine opening remarks. As he started on a special plea, he began, "Your Honor," instead of "Dear God."
— *Fayetta Murray, AR*

I was doing fine on a full page of announcements one Sunday, a bit proud of myself too, when the next announcement about a Pot Luck dinner came out "Pot Lick." There were quite a few giggles, but I corrected it and went on. People had such fun with my "Blooper" that every time there is a Pot Luck dinner to be announced, it is referred to as "Pot Lick".

— *Vollie Sorrellis, TN*

As a young preacher before the video camera in Sermon Delivery Class, I took Matthew 4 as my text. Coming to verse 5, I got my "tang tongueled" and said "Then the devil took Him into the holy City; and he had Him stand on the TENTACLE of the PIMPLE!" instead of the PENTACLE of the TEMPLE. Try to imagine that one.

— *Jeff Lovett, OK*

I was trying to make a point that lack of communication is the major cause of divorce, but somehow things got mixed up and I said "marriage" was the main cause of divorce.

— *Mike Suiter, TX*

One Sunday morning while preaching a "Fire and Brimstone" sermon on moral issues, our P.A. system picked up a trucker saying "That's a big 10-4 buddy."

— *Robert Davis, OH*

An elder was speaking to the congregation comparing the mother's tender love for her infant son to

God's love for us. He said "She bathes him and boils him in oil."

— *Beth Anderson, CA*

Preaching from:
Matthew 5: "A hill set on a city cannot be hid."
Matthew 12: "as Jonah was in the welly of the bell."
Matthew 2: "they offered unto him gifts, gold, and Frankenstein."

— *Robert Calray, AZ*

During a Confirmation service, referring to the new converts, the pastor asked for the 5 new "convicts" to come to the front of the church. He never knew what he said, but several people had to leave the building because they were laughing so hard.

— *Linda Underwood, NE*

In Bible class, someone asked, "Proverbs says not to loan money to a stranger. What about our brethren, are they considered strangers?" I replied. "Well, I have known some strange brethren!"

— *Marvin Greene, KS*

The preacher was thrilled, as a man he had worked with a long time came forward to be baptized. The man was 6'4" and about 240 lbs. As the preacher lifted him out of the baptismal water, he felt his back go out. The faithful new Christian's first act was to carry his preacher out of the water.

— *Virgil Dondlinger, OK*

I heard of a preacher who was unable to climb out of the baptistry because he flooded his waders while bending over to lift a new convert up from the water.

— *Tom Nordic, NC*

While in a Bible class, the minister announced "Tonight's lesson is Money Doesn't Buy Happiness." Having been unemployed for some time, I thought out loud, "No, but it sure makes your misery more tolerable." The preacher replied "Boy, you just ruined my whole lesson."

— *Marvin Green, KS*

As I awoke during a sermon the pastor said, "Where the scriptures speak, we speak. Where the scriptures are silent, we sleep."

— *Sandra Bedlan, AR*

While studying the intricate dress of the priests in the Old Testament, the preacher came to the part that describes how the priests put bells on the bottom of their robes. He asked "Why do you suppose the priests had to tinkle?" After a second of silence, the class broke up with laughter.

— *Gloria O'Rourke, MT*

As a young preacher still in Bible college, I was invited to preach in my home congregation during spring break. I chose to preach on "Consistency." All went well until I began speaking about proper dress. I said "You Christian ladies wouldn't think about parading around in a mini skirt, yet some of you think it's fine to play tennis in skirts that go all the way up to your ____ !" I caught myself in time to say, "Well, you know where they go to."

— Marvin Greene, KS

In Kansas, many preachers are also farmers and ranchers. During one sermon, a preacher-rancher was so preoccupied with the new pickup truck he was buying the next day, he said "pickup" for no reason in the middle of his sermon. He returned to the scriptures after it dawned on him what he had done. Needless to say, he was a little embarrassed, not to mention his wife.

— John Hamm, KS

An elder, presenting a young woman who needed money for her summer mission work, referred to her recent employment as a candy stripper (instead of striper).

— John Hamm, KS

The preacher was trying to explain where a certain place was located, and he said "Not even God knows where this place is."

— Don Heinrichs, RI

Instead of saying the prodigal son ate "with the hogs", he said the prodigal son ate "like a hog."

— Ralph Lichti, TN

The preacher, walking slowly up to the podium, said, "Woke up with a nag this morning." What he meant was, he woke up with a nagging back ache, but the congregation cut loose.

— *Marie Straite, AR*

The preacher changed his topic midway through his sermon and didn't know it until someone told him later. The funny thing is, the preacher's wife didn't notice!

— *Mary Simpson, MN*

While describing the newest addition to a family, the preacher said "The baby weighed 18 pounds and was 7 inches long."

— *Al Kenly, WA*

The lesson topic was earthly possessions and how we put too much value on them. My husband was listing some of these possessions such as money, fancy homes, recreational toys, and even living possessions such as pets. He said "Yes, even our pets can sometimes have more value than they should. But what am I talking about, when I sleep with a dog!" Suddenly there was a heavy silence. He thought to himself "I wonder if anyone thinks I was referring to my wife?" He cautiously looked across the room and there were a couple of people holding in some pretty explosive laughs. He quickly said, "No, No, I don't mean my wife, I mean Jo Jo, our dog!" Too late.

— *Gloria O'Rourke, MT*

The sermon was about throwing all your alcoholic beverages into the river. The next song was "Shall We Gather at the River?"

— Paula Nelson, OR

While talking about parents letting go of the apron strings, the speaker said "overproductive parents," instead of "overprotective" parents.

— Mike Westerfield, NE

Twin sisters were placing membership at a local church and they were introduced as the "sin twisters."

— Delbert Steider, AZ

Trying to be creative, I started "advertising" my next sermon on the Second Coming of Christ. I had little signs taped on doors, ceilings, the sidewalk, etc., that said "He's Coming!" In my enthusiasm, I got a clever idea of sending every family of the congregation a note which had no return address that simply said "He's Coming!" I thought all I had to do on Sunday was step into the pulpit and say, "In case you haven't heard, He's coming!" It lost its effectiveness when one of the widows became concerned and called the police.

— Riley L. Walker, IL

With a sermon on "Some Things for a Christian to Remember," on my mind, I turned on the water to fill the baptistry, which was directly behind the pulpit. Turning it on and off required a trip downstairs to the other end of the building, and it had no overflow valve.

As I began, "This morning I want you to remember…" I heard the splashing of the water behind me. Immediately it dawned on me what I had done. "Oh, no, I didn't remember to turn off the water in the baptistry! Someone turn it off, quick!" Some believed I had planned the whole thing.

— Riley L. Walker, IL

The preacher was speaking about how we view sin. He said "We look at it, we tolerate it, then we embrace it." He used an illustration about a woman who was an alcoholic. She was visiting a friend that had left a bottle of wine on the table. The friend had to answer the phone in another room, and while she was gone, the alcoholic became very nervous. She decided to take the cork out of the bottle and just smell the wine. That caused her so much stress that she jumped up and started walking back and forth in the room trying to get her composure. When the preacher got to the point where she walked back and forth, he said, "She walked up and forth, down and around." After the service, one of the brethren said to the preacher, "I thought I would have to get you a road map to get that lady straightened out."

— Joe K. Alley, TN

The shortest prayer I ever heard a preacher pray was "Dear God, you know our thoughts, Amen."

— Chris Nieman, ND

A young preacher where I worshipped several years ago stated that "...man was created as a free male agent..."

— *Calvin Seitter, OK*

During a Wednesday night adult Bible class, I made a reference to Genesis 13:12, mentioning that Lot "pitched his tent toward Sodom," only it didn't come out that way. I actually said Lot "pinched his tit towards Sodom." The mouths of most people in the class dropped open, while a couple of ladies blurted out laughing. When I realized what I had said, I quickly tried to correct it, only to make the same mistake again for emphasis. Everyone died laughing then, and I died with embarrassment!

— *Name withheld by request*

During a panel discussion about how important preacher's wives were in their husband's ministries, one preacher said "Any woman who wants to be a preacher's wife should be committed." After a short pause he rephrased that, "should be dedicated."

— *Clay Mayland, AR*

Arriving at the gravesight I recited the 23rd Psalm. A dear friend there to assist me, began his prayer... "Will you prease play with me?", uh uh, "Will you play with me prease?", uh uh, "Bow your heads."

— *John Dale, KY*

One of our Elders died and I was trying to convey the thought that those of us who are younger owe a great debt to the older soldiers who have "Blazed the Trail." I said "who have trazed the blails," "trailed the blaze," then finally "blailed the trazes." Whereupon I went on to something I could pronounce, like the benediction.

— *John Dale, KY*

I did a funeral once and said the deceased "died of...death."

— *Al Shonka, MN*

One of our Country Western-loving Elders was a song director. One Sunday morning he introduced a deacon to lead in prayer. He said "After the singing of this song, we'll be led in prayer by 'Little Jimmy Dickens'."

— *Letha Silvy, KY*

I was in a service once where the preacher said, "Will you bow with me as we start the show, I mean the service."

— *Clarence Baker, AR*

While preaching on James 3:4, "Behold also the ships, which though they be so great, and are driven of fierce winds, yet are they turned about with a very small helm." I wanted to use an "updated" word for the King James version rendering of helm. What I wanted to say was "rudder," but what came out was "udder," which has quite a different meaning. After the services, one of the members who got a chuckle out of my "Blooper," said that my sermon was an "udder" catastrophe.

— David Markwell, GA

As a nervous young preacher, slightly unprepared, I referred to Matt., 11:16. As I preached, referring to Jesus causing the lepers to be cleansed as one of his miracles, I called them "leapers," much to the delight of the crowd!

— David Markwell, GA

I was at a funeral where the priest was delivering the eulogy. He went on and on about how good the deceased was, what a terrific mother, whose kids were always clean and so well behaved, etc., etc. The only problem was, I knew the deceased, and she didn't have any children.

— Cortney Nixon, NE

Our Christmas service started with the youth minister and some of the children singing carols. While delivering the sermon, which was about the birth, death, and resurrection of Christ, he came to the baptism of Jesus and said ever so sincerely, "...and the Holy Spirit descended from heaven in the form of a turtledove..." (instead of a dove.) He promptly realized his "blooper," and decided to finish it with a bang, and said, "No, make that two turtledoves and a partridge in a pear tree!"

— J. Jaye Hackney, WA

One of the worst blizzards of the year hit one Sunday morning. I certainly didn't expect anyone to show up for church. Low and behold, one farmer trudged his way to the front door of the church and came in and sat down. Well, by golly, since he went to all the trouble to come to church, I was going to give him my sermon, in all its splendor. After I was finished he said "Thanks for the sermon pastor, but you know if I just had one cow come home, I'd feed her, but I wouldn't give her the whole bale of hay."

— *JD Scamehorn, NE*

One Elder of the Church was introducing the guest speaker and he said that he was from "Corpus Chrispi, Texas."

— *Al Kenly, WA*

The preacher was talking about the women of the Old Testament and remarked about the number of children some of them had. He said some of them were real "Fertile Myrtles."

— *JD Scamehorn, NE*

The pastor was talking about Simon Peter and his relationship with Jesus when without realizing it, referred to him as "Simple Simon."

— *Harold Ahrens, NH*

I was listening to a sermon when Pastor said, "My God, My God, why hast thou forsooken me?"

— *Andria Anderson, FL*

A preacher was talking about how married couples should avoid lumping household tasks into "men" chores and "women" chores. He said, "After all, most women can rake a lawn, and guys, anyone is capable of using a bust duster." We think he meant "dust buster," but maybe there's some new chore we've never heard of!
— *Sara Dinkleman, NE*

This past Sunday, our minister said in a sermon on Matthew 6:25-34... "In His letter, Jesus wrote...!" I didn't know Jesus wrote any letters.
— *Susan Ernst, CT*

One Sunday as our pastor was praying for the sick of our congregation, it came time to be more specific, he said, "And God, especially be with...uh...uh...uh... you know who I mean." He had forgotten their names.
— *Todd Allinder, MN*

I heard a burned out preacher say, "I love the Church, it's the brethren I can't stand!"
— *Sue Beatty, OR*

There was a preacher who left the church and opened up a tobacco store and called it, "HOLY SMOKES".
— *Homer Barber, AZ*

I was listening to a sermon once and the preacher said "Jesus was revived," instead of resurrected.
— *Steve Heinz, TN*

My brother-in-law, who is a preacher, was announcing the names of people who were on the prayer list. He mentioned that one lady will be entering the hospital this week for a "vasectomy," (instead of a hysterectomy). It was after the services when he became aware of his blooper.

— Reeta Baker, VT

I was listening to a sermon that made reference to ball players and the preacher referred to Michael Jordan as Michael Jackson.

— Name withheld because he didn't want to embarrass his pastor

In an effort to impress the men of the congregation with her knowledge of sports, our female pastor referred to "Magic Bird" instead of "Magic Johnson" or "Larry Bird," and "Walt Chamberlain" instead of "Wilt."

— Same as above

The preacher was so engrossed in his presentation concerning the crucifixion of Jesus that he said, "And Mary looked up at Jesus and said, 'My God, My God, why hast thou forsaken me?'" Then he said, "I'm sorry, Mary didn't say that, Jesus did. I mean Jesus said that to God." He started over.

— Annette Brewer, KS

I fell asleep listening to a tape of my own sermon.
— Floyd Lindquist, MA
(I've heard you preach)

At our church, a special plea was given about the never ending heat. The preacher started the prayer by saying, "God it's hot!" instead of something a little gentler.

— *Linda Larson, FL*

How about the preacher who exhorted so fervently about the "fiery darts" of Satan, that he reversed the "f" and "d".

— *Marvin Green, KS*

Not knowing exactly how to say "Jesus rode into Jerusalem on his ass," the preacher got twisted and said, "Jesus rode into Jerusalem on his donkey's ass."

— *Name withheld by request*

I heard of a preacher referring to the Cross as the "Big T," and Jesus and his apostles as "JC and the Boys."

— *Sue Curran, NE*

From the altar in a revival, our evangelist asked that all Christians come forward and pray with the "Seekers." He meant to say, "except for those who have a baby in their lap," or "are holding one in their arms," but he confusingly said, "Unless you are having a baby."

— *Ernie Thomas, IN*

Our pastor announced that he was taking his sermon text from Acts 14, and his co-text from James 2.

After services, he mentioned to me that he realized it sounded like he said "Kotex."

— *Ernie Thomas, IN*

One of the best "Bloopers" I ever heard occurred one Sunday when our rather pompous and very "impressed with himself" minister was giving a memory story. He meant to say, "Back when I was a child," but he actually said, "Back when I was God!" It was a beautiful Freudian slip that fit the man perfectly. It was also on a live radio broadcast.

— *Donald Cooper, OK*

In my church it is customary for the person who presides at the communion service to say a few words about the crucifixion or read a Bible passage about the Cross. One Sunday, an older gentleman in charge talked so long about the death, burial, and resurrection of Jesus, one could have mistaken it for the sermon. After about 12 minutes, and many squirming people, he finally finished and proceeded with the communion.

After this, the preacher got up to do his sermon and said, with a note of gentle reproach, "Well, since Bro. so-n-so already used up half my time, I'll only give you two of the four points in my sermon."

— *Al Kenly, WA*

I was at a church picnic and the pastor, who loved to eat, asked if I had brought my coconut cream pie (his favorite). I told him no, that I hadn't had time to make one. He said, "That's OK, I still love you. Not as much, but I still love you."

I'm not sure, but I think he was serious.

— *Ernestine Baker, KS*

A few years ago, I was asked to be a guest speaker at a neighboring church. I met with the liturgist in the Pastor's study, put on my robe, and with much dignity, took my place at the front of the sanctuary. When it came time for my reading of the scriptures, I stood and flipped my mike cord out of the way as I walked to the lectern. Halfway there, my left leg refused to come along because the cord did a half-hitch around my ankle. It was too late to act as if nothing had happened, so I very carefully removed the obstacle.

Since this act was definitely not in the order of worship, I said, "It is very evident to me you folks have a line on the preacher."

— *Orus Rupe, IN*

While attending a funeral of a friend, our pastor asked us to bow in silent prayer and consider our own morality.

— *Ned Erks, CO*

Our preacher said, "I wish I had a pornographic memory to help me remember the scriptures better."

—*Harold Klepper, CO*

My husband was preaching one Sunday and instead of saying how our lives shine brightly, he said, "shine-ly brights."

— *Bettye Jo Hamm, KS*

On a live television interview, the subject was about forgiveness, and the text was Romans 3:23, "...for all have sinned and fall short of the glory of God." One of the panel said, "Thanks be to God that delivers us from our falling shorts."

— Harold Billings, OK

There was a fund drive at a church where the associate pastor was in charge of half the congregation. He thought it appropriate to have a number of T-shirts printed with a special slogan. This would help increase the amount of money raised and at the same time boost the morale of his group.

At the end of the service, he stood up and raised one of the T-shirts in the air to show to the entire church, and it read...I UPPED MY PLEDGE — UP YOURS!

— Harold Billings, OK

Our pastor was delighted that our small congregation was growing and encouraged us to invite our neighbors to church. One morning, his exuberance got the better of him. Having just toured the newly renovated nursery, he spoke about it from the pulpit, going into great detail about its large size and amenities.

"I'm concerned that it isn't full," he concluded. "So what I'd like for all of you to do this afternoon is to get together with your neighbors and work on filling the nursery."

— Contributed by Bill R. Wise
Reprinted with permission from the
November 1992 Reader's Digest.
© 1992 by the Reader's Digest Assn., Inc.

On Mother's Day our pastor said, "Today we are not only going to honor the oldest mother and the youngest mother, but every single mother."

— *Robert Dickson, NE*

The sermon was about counting your blessings. The preacher said, "Don't ever wish your wife away." What he meant to say was "Don't ever wish your life away."

— *Randy Dubas, AZ*

The pastor was talking about the church in Anchor, Anchorage. What he meant to say was Anchorage, Alaska.

— *Pam Dyer, FL*

While I was preaching a "fire and brimstone" sermon, and getting used to my first set of dentures at the same time...they fell out.

— *Dean Daniels, MO*

I was listening to a sermon when the pastor said something about how cold the weather was, and he said "The low dippy down to around 30."

— *Deena Deprez, PA*

Pastor was talking about the three Presidential candidates "ducking" it out...instead of "duking" it out.

— *Bill Dunham, MO*

When I was living in Ohio, my wife and I attended a Gospel Meeting that was being held by a personal friend who was a powerful preacher.

As our friend was "waxing eloquent" and dealing with moral issues, he started talking about "tight knit" dresses that had just come in style. He said, "Speaking of morality and lust, just take a look at those TIGHT TIT DRESSES!"

Everyone laughed, although he didn't know why. He proceeded and said the very same thing again. "Now just take a look at those TIGHT TIT DRESSES, and tell me they don't excite a man!"

It was after services were dismissed that he found out what he had said. He was embarrassed but thought it over and said, "Well, I'm still right about it!"

— *Dave Reppart, NE*

Our former pastor always enjoyed visits from the members of the congregation. One evening, when he had been feeling under the weather, a family stopped by to chat. A few days later they came over again. In expressing thanks for the previous visit, he said, "You don't know how I felt when you people left the other night!"

— *Robert J. Pietraszek*
Reprinted with permission from
the Nov. 1990 Reader's Digest.
© 1990 by the Reader's Digest Assn., Inc.

One Sunday morning, our minister asked members to stay after the service so he could pick our brains about an upcoming event. He was quick to add, "It should only take a minute."

— *Melody Rebenstorf*
Reprinted with permission from
the Oct. 1990 Reader's Digest
© 1990 by the Reader's Digest Assn., Inc.

In the course of his sermon, our minister referred to the Old Testament story of Balaam and his talking donkey. He explained that God made the donkey talk, and he added "The donkey was God's 'Better Business Burro'."

— *John Able, AZ*

My dad was giving a lesson prayer. He was also taking the opportunity to explain how to use the concordance in the back of the Bible.

He explained that a person could look up a word and would be given a list of scriptures where the word appears. He told the audience that the list would also include a phrase containing the word, but the word would be abbreviated to only the first letter. Then he gave this example: "Here in the concordance under the heading 'pray' we find this scripture. 'If anyone has troubles, let him p _ _ _ '."

(How about p _ _ _ without ceasing.)

— *Tammy Cecil, NE*

While introducing a new member to the congregation the preacher said... "This is Patty ___. She looks just like her older sister who is already a member here, only a smaller virgin."

— *Tammy Cecil, NE*

All winter long the church roof leaked. Members had to strategically avoid the unwanted water when choosing their seats. Spring finally came and the roof was repaired except for the overhang above the entry way.

One Sunday the entire church was full and some latecomers were standing by the front door looking for a place to sit.

The pastor said, "It's wonderful seeing everyone here today. Except for a few drips by the front door we're ready for a great year!"

— *Donovan Hinze, OK*

After seeing the collection totals for the month, our pastor said that he wishes the government would quit printing $1 bills.

— *William Suda, VA*

Our preacher was talking about traveling on the train and said "AMWAY" train instead of "AMTRAK".

— *Ken Alley, NE*

I heard of a minister, in the middle of a marriage ceremony, backing up two steps and falling into a floor level baptistry. (Splish, splash, I was taking a bath...)
— *Laura Reppart, NE*

HEY, SEND ME YOUR STORIES!

Chapter 2

Out of the Mouths of Kiddos

My 12-year-old son told me that one of his baseball teammates was baptized last Sunday. He wondered if God would help his friend with his pitching now.
(Couldn't hurt.)

— *Brien Alley, NE*

As my young grandson and I were driving home from our Lutheran Church service, we passed another church which was located by a busy pedestrian crosswalk. There was a warning sign on the corner that he read slowly to me, "Watch...out...for... Presbyterians."

— *Pat Brem, NE*

Before the church collection, a man read from the Scriptures, "Do you have any idea what I have done for all of you?" A little kid hollered, "Yeah!"

— *Al Kenyon, WA*

The primary Bible History class was reviewing the lesson on Creation. It was already established that on the sixth day God created Adam and Eve. The teacher then asked, "How did God create both Adam and Eve?" A first grader confidently and sincerely answered, "Naked!"

— *Linda Baker, NE*

I have a friend whose 4-year-old daughter, Amy, would pray at night, "Now I Amy down to sleep...."

— *Mary Meyer, NE*

When I was a kid, my brother and I would always look forward to singing the hymn "LOW IN THE GRAVE" in church. We sang it this way: "Up from the grave He arose, with a great big booger in His nose." Mom always punished us afterward, but it was a lot of fun.

— *Harry Lisle, TX*

At church camp this summer, several young people were baptized. Walking back to the cabins one evening, I overheard one 7-year-old girl say that she wanted to be baptized, too. Her counselor remarked that this was wonderful, but that she was probably too young to completely understand about being baptized. The girl responded, "Oh, yes, I do! All you have to do is say 'yes, yes, yes,' to all the questions, hold your nose, and don't breathe when they put you under the water."

— *Bettye Jo Hamm, KS*

Our guest speaker said at the beginning of his sermon, "I'm going to preach on 'root', not 'fruit'!"

His little three-year-old daughter hollered from the pew, "Oh, no! Not again!"

— *Mary Jones, MO*

During a lesson on sharing, the Sunday school teacher pinched a piece of cookie off and gave it to a little kid. The next in line, a husky boy, said "I'm a lot bigger so I'll need a bigger piece."

— *Karen Palik, NE*

My child came home from church and told me that they sang a song about a "crossed-eyed bear named Gladly." (Cross I bear gladly.)

— *Ann Barwick, NJ*

Ever heard a song about "Gravy Rose?" (Up from the grave He arose.)

— *Ann Barwick, NJ*

A smart alec's turn to say grace: "Rub a dub, dub. Thanks for the grub. Yea God!"

— *Jim Fischer, OK*

While showing how a mother bird pushed the young offspring out of the nest to make them fly, the preacher made motions and said "chirp, chirp, chirp," to emphasize the setting. A cute three-year-old took off on that, and chirped the rest of the service.

— *Mildred Barth, KS*

A girl, about 13 years old, slowly dragged her five-year-old sister down the aisle to me during the invitation song. I thought they were going to use the bathroom in back of the baptistry. They stood right in front of me and didn't move. I told them to have a seat, and asked the older girl, "Why do you come?" She said, "I brought my friend to Jesus." That's exactly what I told the congregation.

— *Robert Calbray, AZ*

I saw a toddler taken out of church for discipline eight times, and yes, it was the pastor's kid.

— *Mini Fitzgerald*

One kid's addition to the hymn, "I Was Sinking Deep in Sin, Weeeeeeeeeeeeee."

— *Ray Field, MT*

"All who are prepared, come to the Lord's Table." One kid said "Why not say, soup's on?"

— *Karen Palik, NE*

A father's annoying joke of poking his yawning kid's tongue, abruptly ended in the middle of a church service after his finger went too far, the kid gagged, and then threw up all over the floor.

— *Larry Axtell, NC*

In the children's Christmas play, Joseph asked the innkeeper if they had any room. The innkeeper said, "No, we have no room...." He forgot his next line but improvised by saying…"but, why don't you come on in and have a drink."

— *Sandra Fenning, AR*

While attending a funeral where the remains were cremated, they were put in an urn, wrapped, and presented to the family. My four-year-old niece turned to me and said, "Who gets to open the present?"

— *Peg Waldemade, NE*

During church, my granddaughter was staring at my "spider looking" varicose veins on my leg and said, "Where did you get those tattoos?"

— *Esther Monnier, NE*

During a processional at our church, as a large flag was being carried down the center aisle, my two-year-old son hollered out, "Look, Mom, a fag!"

— *Sara Dinkelman, NE*

While teaching a Sunday school class for preschoolers, I observed one little girl wiping her nose on her sleeve. Making this exceptionally gross was the large booger deposited at the end of her sleeve. I said, "Jennifer, where does that go?" (meaning on a kleenex.) She looked at the booger for a moment, picked it up and stuck it back in her nose.

— *Bettye Jo Hamm, KS*

Finding her three-year-old son too much to handle in church services, the mom grabbed him one last time and sat him down rather hard on the pew. He hollered out, "Mom, you broke my balls!" The silence that followed is one that I hope I never have to experience. A short time later he reached into his back pockets and pulled out two smashed ping pong balls.

— *Bettye Jo Hamm, KS*

My niece's daughter Lacy, about 4 years old, sang in the Little Kids Choir. After a concert, my niece told her to "sing out" next time so we could hear her better.

At the next concert, we sat in the balcony to listen and after the first song, Lacy hollered, "Hey Mom, can you hear me up there?"

— *Mervell Bumgarner, NE*

As the priest was finishing communion and wiping out the chalice, my son said, "Can we go when he gets the dishes done?"

— *Edna Edgerley, NE*

As I returned to my seat after partaking of the communion, my four-year-old asked, "What did you get to eat this time?"

—*Jessie Nelson, FL*

A young newcomer to a Catholic service noticed people were kneeling before they sat down and asked what they were doing. The friend told her it's called a "genuflect." The youngster said, "Why don't they just call it a squat?"

— *Mary Alley, NE*

When asked if he had a real Christmas tree or a fake one the child answered, "We have a real one, like the Bible says."

— Jeff Stalings, OH

I was sitting behind a little girl when she leaned over the back of her pew and threw up all over me.

— Eileen Miller, TN

I was standing for the closing prayer when a toddler in front of me lifted up his mom's skirt from behind, and she didn't know it.

— Milton Sprock, OH

Preacher doing the kid's sermon: "What has brown fur, a bushy tail, and collects nuts?" He called on one kid that said, "I know the answer is Jesus, but it sure sounds like a squirrel to me!"

— Linda Underwood, NE
(From a Paul Harvey broadcast)

The little boy's mother slipped into his bedroom while he was on his knees during prayer. She was just in time to hear "Lord, did you see Bro. Baker walking with his eyes closed during the last prayer? He walked right into the wall when he was going to the back to greet people. Didn't you think that was funny?"

— Karen Pittard, TN

One little boy turned to his dad when the preacher got up to begin his sermon and said, "I hate this part."

— *Harold Mitchell, NE*

Another little boy came up to the preacher and said, "Your sermons are boring and confusing." Thanks, I needed that.

— *Harold Mitchell, NE*

The kid forgot that he had to recite the 23rd Psalm that night at church. All Sunday afternoon he crammed it into his head. He was so pre-occupied with it that when the phone rang, he answered it "The Lord is my Shepherd."

— *Al Kenly, WA*

Right in the middle of a church service, the nipple came off a baby's bottle, spewing milk everywhere. The parents were trying to mop up the mess with whatever was handy, but not having too much success. As the usher was passing the collection plate, another of their youngsters said loudly, "Hey, mister, my sister spilled her milk, do you have a towel?" At the end of the service, the pastor was shaking hands with the dad, and asked "Are you the family that needed the towel?"

— *Gary Groteluschen, NE*

I was sitting in the front row with my outspoken three-year-old listening to a missionary speak on the

Lord's work in Africa. The missionary apologized for his speech, which was somewhat mumbled because of a case of shingles he had on his face. My youngster asked, "Why that man talk funny?" I told him to shush, I'd tell him after church. "But, Mom, he talks so funny, how come?" On and on and on, until he said loudly, "Mom, he says ba, bla, ba, bla, ba, bla." The missionary heard this and stared at me until I shrunk. I've never been so embarrassed in my life.

— *JoAnn Groteluschen, NE*

It was my turn to recite the memory verse for the pastor. I said, "He that heareth me, heareth you, and uh, uh, uh," (I couldn't remember the rest), so I said "He that heareth you, heareth me." The pastor whispered to me, "Despiseth." "Oh yeah, He that despiseth me, despiseth you."

— *Linda Underwood, NE*

It was a Christmas service and there was a Nativity scene by the altar. The priest asked all the little children to come up to the front to see it. He asked the question, "What should be done to keep the baby Jesus warm?" One child said to put him in a blanket, another said to put straw around the manger, but the third child responded, "Shut the door!"

— *Dean Fredericks, NE*

During the communion service, a four-year-old boy was giving his mom trouble about not letting him have any of the "cracker" that was being passed around. He said, "OK, but when the Kool-Aid man comes by, I want some!"

— *Mary Swanson, ID*

While standing in line receiving communion during a mass, my husband was behind me holding our 15-month-old son. He was asleep, but having outbursts of laughter like he was dreaming of something funny. I turned around to see what was going on, (I thought my husband was tickling him), but decided there was nothing we could do. He would start, then stop, then start again. People were starting to get amused, and we knew things were getting out of control when the priest started to laugh. We were so embarrassed.

— *Barb Fiegener, NE*

When my son was little, I had a difficult time controlling him in church. During one Sunday service, in order to keep him occupied, I decided to let him take the strings out of my shoes. He had so much fun taking them out and putting them back in, I thought I had discovered something at last! Toward the end of the sermon, I looked over at him and didn't see my strings anywhere. He had thrown them out into the center aisle and was laughing with the people that saw him do it.

— *Mollene Gergen, NE*

A normally passive little guy seemed distressed and was naughty all through the service. The parents had no idea what the problem was until after the service and the kid told them he didn't get to wear his cowboy boots to church, but daddy got to wear his!

— *Paul Rucker, TX*

Before the service, the elementary age kids were having a sing-along in the front of the church. One by one, a child would start singing his favorite song and the rest would join in. All went well until one boy started to sing, "When you're out of Schlitz, you're out of beer," and the others joined in.

— *Eva Deterding, NE*

The teacher was talking to her pre-school class about how Jesus will take your sins away. My four-year-old nephew said, "When will Jesus give them back?" She said, "He never does."

My nephew replied, "That not very nice, take something and not give it back."

— *Shirley Knorr, NE*

While tending one of my pre-schoolers during a sermon, my other toddler got away from me. By the time I looked back to check, he had walked down the aisle and sat on the step in front of the preacher, sucking his thumb and holding on to his blanket!

— *Mollene Gergen , NE*

A little girl used to sit with me during services. One Sunday during the sermon, she started going through my purse, like she always did, looking for something to play with. She looked up at me and said, "I wish you had something in your purse besides dirty kleenex's."

— *Lydia Romanowski, NE*

Caught up in the singing of, "Hide it under a bushel, No! I'm going to let it shine," one exuberant child sang, "Hide it under a bush, HELL NO! I'm going to let it shine." The teacher had a hard time taking the wind out of his sail.

—*Eva Deterding, NE*

One little girl couldn't understand why they would write a church song about "Bringing in the Sheets."

— *Martha Benning, GA*

While preaching a sermon the pastor noticed people in the last rows looking down at the floor. He didn't think much about it until the "wave" started coming forward with each pew of people looking down. Eventually, out from under the first pew came his one-year-old, who had gotten away from his mom and crawled under all the pews on his way to the front.

— *JD Scamehorn, NE*

We were taking turns reading from the Old Testament in our Bible class. It was one boy's turn to read about the priests in the synagogue. This word was new to him but he did his best by sounding it out, "sin-a-go-gue."

— *Steve Ferguson, NE*

My five-year-old daughter kept telling us about Adam and Steve in her Sunday school class. It took a while before we figured out she meant Adam and Eve.

— *Dave Mettenbrink, NE*

A young mother was tugging her newly-potty-trained daughter down the aisle. The mother wasn't paying much attention because the reason her daughter wouldn't come gently is because her panties were down by her ankles. She didn't like them and by golly, she wasn't going to wear them!

— *Bruce Tandy, NE*

In the middle of a church service, a little girl about 4 took off running through the pews. The dad got up and ran after her and suddenly it became a game of chase me and catch me. As soon as she was almost caught, she would duck under a couple of pews and escape. She out-maneuvered her dad until the preacher asked for help.

— *Bruce Tandy, NE*

I used to enjoy sitting behind a certain little boy to see how many people he hit with his Cheerios.

— *Dick Parne, TX*

It was Easter Sunday Mass and during the service the priest was walking down the aisle throwing holy water over the congregation. My three-year-old got hit and said, "Hey, who spit on me?"

— *Norma Olsen, PA*

A five-year-old farm boy, sitting next to me in church, exclaimed about a freckled faced boy passing by: "Hey, look at that Brockled-face kid." (A Brockled-faced cow has a similar sprinkled color scheme on its face.)

— *Irene Kramer, NE*

As a little kid tried to toss his quarter in the collection plate, it missed and fell to the floor, making quite a ruckus. Another kid close by said loudly, "Air ball!"

— *Brien Alley, NE*

A little girl threw up in Sunday school class, and a rather crude classmate said, "Who wants to figure out what she had for breakfast!"

— *Brien Alley, NE*

As an usher passing the collection plate one Sunday, I waited while a couple who had given their daughter a dime struggled to get her to let go of it. As they pried it from her fingers, she angrily yelled, "I don't see why I have to pay anything, I didn't want to come here anyway!"

— *Clarance Hoffman, NE*

I was so proud of my kindergartner singing so fervently in church. I decided to bend down and listen a little closer and heard instead of "Send the light, the blessed gospel light," I heard, "Send the law...."

— *Phyllis Mackey, NE*

We drove by the Grace Lutheran Church the other day and my five-year-old daughter said, "Grace who?"
— *Sandy Peterson, AX*

Years ago my three-year-old cousin was standing on the pew beside me holding his own hymnal when he leaned over and asked, "What channel are we on?"
— *Reeta Baker, VT*

Noticing so many restaurants and stores open on Sunday, my husband and I started reminiscing about when we were kids and how special Sundays were because nobody worked. My six-year-old looked puzzled and asked, "I wonder if working on Sunday makes God mad?"
— *Donna Ostrom, KS*

I was in a health food store when a fellow with long hair, beard, and white robe came in to do some shopping. I could feel my toddler staring at this man, but felt there was nothing I could do about it. All of a sudden the ice broke when my seven-year-old said to her, "No, Regan, it's not God!"
— *Ann Romohr, NE*

During the height of tourist season, I was visiting family in Hot Springs, South Dakota. While attending a packed house at Mass with lots of kids howling and running up and down the aisles, my nine-year-old cousin turned to his mother and said: "Church is a regular whorehouse today, isn't it?" (We hope he meant horror.)
— *James Bormann, NY*

A minister was trying to explain the Lord's Supper to a group of children. He compared it to having a kind of party. He asked the group, "What do people do at your house when there's a party?" Hoping for an answer of "celebrate" or "praise," one kid said, "Go crazy!"

— Jean Hylton, NE

When the bread was being passed during communion, I heard a little child yell, "I want some cake!"

— Jean Hylton, NE

As we were passing the First Christian Church, my kindergartner said, "That's really neat." I asked her what she meant, and she answered, "The first one." I was still confused and asked again what she meant. She said, "Is that church really the first one?"

— Maxine Pettygrove, AZ

When my boys were little, if one of our goldfish died, we would have a little funeral, say the Lord's Prayer, and flush the fish down the toilet. As my boys grew up and had their own families, they carried on the same tradition.

While attending the funeral of my granddaughter's other grandmother, while barely old enough to talk, she said, you guessed it, "Are we gonna flush her?"

— Mollene Gergen, NE

My family always sat in the back of the church during mass. One Sunday my husband had to usher. When the time came for him to go to the altar, he stood up and began his long walk to the front. I took my eye off my three-year-old for one second, and by the time I looked back, he had taken off running after his daddy. I caught up to him right as my husband stopped at the front.

— *Vickie Rommich, NE*

After getting my offering envelope out of my purse, my little son said, "Mommy, Mommy!" I told him to hush because grandpa was about to preach. He kept on and on, until in desperation, I asked him what was the matter. He whispered loudly, "You snapped your purse shut on my finger!" Sure enough, I had.

— *Dorie Baker, Hawaii*

At our church, children walk to the altar and make their contribution. On this particular Sunday, we had a visiting pastor. When my grandson didn't return in his usual time, I asked him, "What took so long?" He answered, "The new pastor was flipping some of the kids double-or-nothing, and it was taking longer."

— *Gerald Voy, NE*

We were in a church service where the preacher asked for a moment of silence so we could reflect on our blessings. When all was quiet and everyone was in silent meditation, some kid whistled "Shave and a Haircut, Two Bits."

— *Melvin Parks, OK*

Our pastor was doing his children's sermon by radio broadcast, and the topic was "Rules." When he asked the children if they have any rules at their houses, one four-year-old piped up and blurted over the P.A. system, "We can't pee in the yard!"

— Donald Cooper, OK

When my son was about six, he and I discussed the resurrection and the meaning of Easter. I explained things the best I could to a lad of his understanding, and he said, "Now I've heard everything."

— Wayne Keller, WA

A new kid joined the second grade at a Catholic school. On the second day, he raised his hand and signaled #1. Sister Christine says, "Mark, you may leave the room." Mark left but was soon back saying, "I can't find it, Sister!"

Sister Christine asked Bernard to go with Mark and help him find it. He and Mark left the room and in five minutes returned and took their seats. Mark was grinning from ear to ear, "We found it Sister, I had my pants on backwards!"

— Cliff Thomas, SD

While reciting the "Hail Mary," my three-year-old friend declared, "Messed up is the fruit in your room." (Blessed is the fruit of your womb.)

— Joygerm Joan, NY

The 4th grade church school was working with acronyms for L.E.N.T. Instead of something like "Let's Eliminate Negative Thinking," David declared: the "Lord Eats Noodles Today."

— Joygerm Joan, NY

I was behind the stage curtain of our Fellowship Hall. I was aware of several kids on the stage steps, but they didn't know I could hear their conversation. One boy, about five, told another of the same age, "Randy thinks you're a nerd!" That phrase caught my attention, and I assumed I would be in the midst of breaking up a quarrel within minutes. However, the statement that followed caused a deafening silence: "What kind of nerd?"

If we each could but measure our responses with such wisdom!

— Jeff Knighton, KS

As a young boy was being dragged out of the service for discipline, he hollered, "Somebody have mercy!"

— Galen Sears, NC

Children's responses:
    Noah's wife was called Joan of Ark.
    The epistles are the wives of the apostles.
    The fourth Commandment is: Humor thy father and
        mother.
    Lot's wife was a pillar of salt by day, and a ball of fire
        by night.
    Eskimos are God's frozen people.

The tower of Babel is where Solomon kept his wives.
When Mary heard she was to be the mother of Jesus, she went off and sang the Magna Carta.
Holy Acrimony is another name for marriage.
The 8th commandment is: Thou shalt not witness thy bare neighbor.
Christians have only one wife. They call it monotony.
Paraffin is next in order to seraphin.
Adam and Eve had twins: Cain and Mable.
The Pope lives in a vacuum.
Iran is the bible of the Moslems.
Samson's wife was Mrs. Samson.
A republican is a sinner mentioned in the Bible.

— *Bill Martin, IN*

I heard of a very strict Mennonite pastor who took his five-year-old son out of church for discipline. The boy thought he was being treated unfairly. Later that day, the pastor took his son to a men's business meeting and made him sit in the corner until the meeting was over.

At this time the boy got his revenge. He said to the group, "My dad will probably deny this, but he smokes sometimes!"

— *Paul Jacobson, CA*

It was a big day in church for my friend; she would go forward and be installed as the new Sunday School Superintendent. She pleaded with her husband to keep their two-year-old quiet during the ceremony. He promised he would.

The installation went perfectly, and all was quiet back in the pew. However, as she walked back to her seat she saw why. Her son had gone through her purse, and was happily, and quietly, twirling a tampon around by the string! Her husband's only response was, "He was quiet, wasn't he?"

— *Linda Underwood, NE*

During a solemn ceremony, as the altar boys lit candles, our three-year-old sang out, "Happy Birthday to you!"

— *Shirley Knorr, NE*

While keeping busy during the sermon, a little boy's toy car rolled away from him, going several pews ahead. Before his mother realized, he had crawled under the pews, through several people's legs and retrieved the car. From five pews ahead, he stood up and hollered, "Mom, I found it!"

— *Shirley Knorr, NE*

A kid pointed to the preacher's head and said, "You got an empty spot up there." What he meant was a "bald spot."

— *Keith Elliot, AR*

While teaching a children's class, the teacher asked the question, "Who wrote the book of Psalms?" One perky kid said "Psalmbody."

— *Karen Palik, NE*

While sitting behind the cutest little boy, all of a sudden I thought I would die when he wiped a booger on his mom's dress.

— *Opal Butzske, MI*

On Lutheran Confirmation day, the pastor asked the question, "Who started the church?" One excited boy eagerly waved his hand, much to his mother's pride, and when called on said, "MARTIN LUTHER KING!" The pastor stopped, the mother melted.

— *Norma Christian, NE*

"There were 12 loaves in 2 dishes."

— *Eric Simpson, SC*

I remember some little kid hollering the song numbers after the song director announced them. It was real funny, for a while.

— *Allen Olson, OR*

The kids were playing church and one said, "Jesus, if you don't behave, I'll have Joseph get the ruler!"

— *Pearl Olson, IN*

Carrying a little one out of church for discipline can make a parent think twice when the kid hollers "Somebody help me!" It's a little different for the mom carrying a child screaming, "I want Daddy!" and "Daddy" is the preacher!

— *Arthur Naber, SC*

A kid says, "If we were made out of the dust of the earth, why don't we turn to mud when we get rained on?"

— Karen Palik, NE

WHAT ARE PASTORS?

He works for God.

He wrote the Bible.

Pastors tell you about Jesus and smile.

They marry people that need it.

He's the bald guy that sings real loud.

They give money to poor people.

We always have to shake his hand after church.

He's the person that does most of the talking at church.

Pastors make my mom happy and my dad mad.

Pastors eat a lot at picnics.

They talk a long time about stuff.

They go to church all the time.

He gets all the money in the plates.

He's the one in the robe that looks like Jesus.

Pastors read the Bible a lot.

Do you mean the preacher? He's the guy that works at the church with the janitor.

— Bob Simon, AZ

While riding quietly in the hearse on the way to bury my husband, my six-year-old grandson said to the driver, "Man, you got a great set of wheels!"

— Yvonne Junge, NE

As I watched a mom force her little son to put his quarter in the collection plate, the boy said, "Mommy, that's mine!"

— Al Kenly, WA

Every time the congregation would finish a song, my youngster (who could barely talk) would start singing. It lasted about six months and everybody got quite a kick out of her.

— Cathy Meyer, NE

I was in a service when a little boy (the pastor's kid) stood on the pew and hollered, "That's enough, Dad!"

— Mrs. Pearson, NE

My four-year-old daughter was sure she could handle going to the bathroom all by herself. About the middle of the communion service, I started wondering if she was taking care of business or not, when I heard a yell from the bathroom, "Mom, I'm done!"

— Bettye Jo Hamm, KS

During a "Pew Packers" session, where the small children answer Bible questions, the teacher asked a little boy named Seth who the first three sons of Adam and Eve were. He could only think of Cain and Abel until the teacher said, "The third one has your name. The boy said, "Cain, Abel, and Seth!"

When the teacher asked the little girl next to him to recite them, she said, "Cain, Abel, and Janie!"

— Bettye Jo Hamm, KS

In the quiet preceding the prayer, my two-year-old farm-raised nephew hollered, "Mom, I got shit on my boots!"

— *Mary Tieken, NE*

A pre-school member of my Sunday school class was not very impressed with the story of Martha anointing Jesus' feet with perfume. He exclaimed, "We put perfume here (pointing to his armpit), not on our feet!" On the way home from Sunday school his father asked him what he had learned that day. He responded that the story had been about some woman putting deodorant on Jesus. His father had some questions for me the next Sunday.

— *Judi Domeier, NE*

After Dad got back from partaking of the Communion wine, my little sister hollered, "Mom, Dad smells like he's been to the club again!"

— *Jenni Reiter, NE*

Every time this elderly man would lead us in prayer, it seemed his pleas would get longer and longer. One Sunday as he prayed, my three-year-old niece got impatient and hollered loudly, "AMEN!"

The whole congregation started laughing and the man concluded his prayer quickly.

— *Alice Thayer, NE*

During the middle of the church service I took my eyes off my toddler son for just a minute, and by the time

I turned back to him, he had taken off his dirty diaper and was standing at the end of the pew about to leave.

— Victoria York, NE

A friend of mine tells of a little girl who attended church with her mother and suddenly began to feel ill.

"Mama," she said, "I have to go throw up."

"Hurry around to the little garden in back of the church," said the parent.

Presently the girl was back and her mother asked "Were you there and back already?"

"Oh, I didn't have to go way out there," replied the tot. "I saw a box in the back of the church which said 'For the sick'."

— Don Russell, NE

Several of my kindergarten students were looking at a picture of Mary and baby Jesus in the manger. One of them asked, "Where's the dad?" Another answered, "He's getting the BBQ started."

— Alice Whitmore, AR

I could tell my three-year-old son was scared as I took him to the doctor to get a bad splinter removed. I told him that it was going to be OK because Jesus was going to be there with him.

As we sat down in the full reception room, he looked up at me and whispered, "Which one's Jesus?"

— Marline Voss, TN

"Job, Psalms, Proverbs,...Enthusiastics."

50

One kid's definition of Lent: "It's the stuff that gets stuck in the dryer thing."

— *Bob Wyman, KS*

While teaching my preschool class about guilt and what it means to do bad things, I asked one child if she felt bad after she disobeyed her mommy. She answered, "No, but it makes my mommy feel bad."

— *Christine Welsh, NC*

As I showed my 1st grade class a picture of Jesus holding up his hands and preaching to his disciples, I asked them what they thought he was saying. One child said, "He's telling them to be good." Another said, "To not be naughty." The third child had a different approach. She said, "He's telling them that he'll be back next Sunday."

— *Edna Watkins, AZ*

As a man with a husky voice read the scriptures from the back of the church instead of the customary front pulpit, my three-year-old said, "Is that God?"

— *Linda Virchow, KY*

I was teaching a kindergarten class a lesson about Jesus dying on the cross, and I asked "Who knows what Jesus said before he died?"

No one said anything for the longest time until one fellow raised his hand and said, "Jesus said, 'Good Luck, everybody'."

— *Katherine Tieken, OK*

After watching a teenager being baptized, my youngest said, "How old do you have to be to be advertised?"

"Be what?" I asked.

He answered, "You know, advertised...like when they put you under the water."

— *Wally Sommerfield, TX*

This little boy always sang, "Jesus loves me, this I know. For the milo tells me so." He lived on a farm.

— *Donald Wagner, AR*

Every kid in class was supposed to use the word "heaven" in a sentence.

The first kid said, "When I die I hope to go to heaven."

The second kid said, "Heaven is where God lives."

The third kid said, "My mom is heaven another headache."

— *Francis Jacobs, FL*

One young fellow almost got them all correct. "Psalms, Proverbs, Ecclesiastes, Song of Salmon."

— *David Hampp, OR*

My three-year-old son and I were looking at the jet streams in the sky and he asked, "Daddy, can we go to heaven on one of those planes?"

— *Charles Irwin, NH*

My six-year-old daughter was asked what church she attended. She thought and said, "I can't remember exactly, but it's one of the Lutheran churches." Later she exclaimed, "I remember now. It's the German Shepherd Lutheran Church!"

— Edgar Jacobs, OK

We took our five-year-old nephew to church for the first time. When communion was being observed, one of the ushers started giving the prayer for the bread. My nephew asked, "What's he doing?" I answered, "We're having the Lord's Supper."

"Oh, good" he said, "I'm hungry."

— Jenny Davis, OK

One kid was happy that she belonged to her church, "cause you don't have to go through a perco-lator to get to heaven like the Catholics do."

— Gary Harrison, AR

A five-year-old's explanation of Creation: "...then God put Adam to sleep and took out a wishbone to make the lady."

— Carl Albrecht, KS

The pre-school class lesson was about the miracle of Jesus feeding the 5000 people with the five loaves and two fish.

The teacher asked, "How do you think Jesus could feed so many people with so little food?"

One child answered, "My mommy makes 'Clean

the Refrigerator Soup' with just a little bit of food, maybe that's what he did."

— *Connie Baker, MN*

I told my son, "No, on Super Bowl Sunday, when the pastor raises his hands to praise God, it doesn't mean 'Touchdown'!"

— *Carl Meyers, MN*

A friend asked my five-year-old what part of church he liked best. He said, "The going home part."

— *Richard Mason, TX*

It was a habit for our family to recite scriptures on the way to church each Sunday morning. When it came time for my youngest daughter to repeat the selected scripture after all the other kids, instead of repeating "Keep your tongue from lies and deceit," she said "Keep your tongue from lice and disease."

— *Ann Fenske, NE*

As I was sitting through a rather lengthy sermon, my daughter's little neighborhood friend who was sitting with us hollered, "I HATE CHURCH AND SO DOES MY DAAAAAAD!"

I thought I was going to die!

— *Jane Meyer, NE*

My daughter was talking to my five-year-old grandson about the meaning of Lent. She asked him what he would like to give up during this period and he thought and thought and finally said, "I think I'll give up Sunday School."

She remarked that that isn't what she meant. He thought again and said, "OK, I'll give up church then."
— *Frank Harre, NE*

As a beautiful white dove flew overhead, my four-year-old daughter asked, "Is that the 'Holy Dove'?"
— *LoriAnn Hughes, AR*

As the chimes rang in our church, my three-year-old son said quietly, "It sounds like Taco Bell."
— *Cathy Howard, MO*

My daughter likes to brag about her pastor daddy going to school at a "cemetery."
— *Nancy Plamann, KS*

Our four-year-old daughter remarked how much she liked "Pom Pom" Sunday.
— *Betty Norvil, AZ*

Noticing a lot of special decorations at our Easter Service, my daughter remarked about how this reminded her of her birthday party.
— *Mary Pelan, AZ*

One kid thought the special name given to the first Wednesday in Lent was "Leap Year."
— *George Dannon, ID*

This kid almost had it right when he said, "I believe in Jesus Christ, the only forgotten Son of God."

— *Jerry Smith, AR*

I asked my grandson if he would like to go to the altar with me. He said, "No, but would you bring me back something to eat?"

— *Marlow Spohn, UT*

While we were waiting in the Communion line, my niece asked, "Isn't there any express lane?"

— *Carla Powell, MN*

As is taught, when we are baptized we become "new creatures in Christ."

One youngster said, "Baptism makes us new animals for God."

— *Kathryn Ingbeitsen, MN*

One little fellow was overheard as singing: "Microwave the boat ashore, alleluia."

— *Robert Dealey, MN*

At this Lutheran church, the question was asked the 1st grade class, "Can anyone name the four Gospels?"

One boy answered, "Matthew, Mark, Luther, and John."

— *Carol Krumbach, MI*

I asked my class why Jesus could do miracles. One boy said, "Because he knew magic."
— *Beverly Siezak, OH*

I showed my class a picture of Jesus and one of them asked why he wasn't smiling. A less than enthusiastic child remarked, "Because he had to go to church again."
— *Eleanor Kassik, TN*

As we parked our car in the church parking lot, I saw the new vicar going into the church. I asked my six-year-old daughter if she knew who that man was. She answered, "Yes, that's the man that wants to be a pastor when he grows up."
— *Loren Novak, SD*

The pastor's first sentence of his sermon was "Lo, I am with you always."
My restless daughter said, "Oh, no. We're going to be here a long time!"
— *Bernice Taylor, AR*

The children's sermon was about "Grudges." The pastor asked the class what a grudge was.
One boy raised his hand and said, "It's where you put the car."
— *Paul Sirber, MA*

The question was asked a kindergarten class "Who was Jesus?" One kid said, "He invented the Bible book."
— *Ann Bartels, AZ*

As my son looked up at the statue of Jesus on the cross, he remarked, "Holy cow, Mom. There's God!"
— *Chris Tonniges, NE*

A seven-year-old boy in my congregation was chosen Student of the Month in his elementary school. Comments about him from his peers included, "His sins-of-humor" is well known.
— *Woody McKay, GA*
From "The Joyful Noiseletter"
Reprinted with permission

As we walked into mass, my daughter looked up at the cross and asked, "Does that T stand for Tonniges?"
— *Chris Tonniges, NE*

The young boy was reciting the books of the Old Testament: "Amos, Obadiah,..." He couldn't remember any more so the teacher gave him this hint. "He was swallowed by a whale," she remarked.
The boy sparked, "Oh yeah! Pinocchio!"
— *Barb Shearer, NE*

I have a friend whose young son took a straw out of her purse while she wasn't looking. As she listened to the sermon, he held it loosely in the palm of one hand, and by smacking one end with the other hand, launched it into the lap of an unsuspecting worshipper, three rows ahead.
— *Ann Fenske, NE*

One kid said Mary's husband was named Virg. "Yes," he said, "Virg 'n Mary!"

One Sunday my three-year-old daughter was sitting on my lap. She was just learning how to zip, snap, button, etc., and she was fiddling with the buttons on my blouse during the sermon. Of course, I was keeping half an eye on her, but I soon realized that she wasn't having any success, so I devoted my attention to the sermon.

After the lesson, the congregation rose and I stood and shifted my daughter to one hip. We were only a few rows from the front of the church, so Pastor had a clear view of us from the stage. He was trying to be discreet, but I could tell he was sending me an urgent message with his eyes pointedly staring at me! I felt a little uncomfortable, wondering what it could be, until I finally realized my little girl had learned how to button (or should I say UN-button) and my entire blouse was gaping open.

Pat Brinkman, NE

My young son was watching the people in our congregation go up to the front for communion. He asked me why they were doing this and what does communion mean. I explained to him that this was a very special way of remembering that Jesus had suffered for us all by being nailed to the cross and dying for our sins. This made him look very sober, and then he asked earnestly, "Well, where were the policemen?"

Pat Brinkman, NE

HEY, SEND ME YOUR STORIES!

Chapter 3

Out of the Mouths of Typewriters

This afternoon there will be meetings in the south and north ends of the church. Children will be baptized at both ends.

Tuesday at 4 p.m. there will be an ice cream social. All ladies giving milk, please come early.

The Ladies Liturgy Society will meet on Wednesday. Mrs. Johnson will sing "Put Me in My Little Bed" accompanied by the pastor.

Thursday at 5 p.m. there will be a meeting of the Little Mother's Club. All those wishing to become little mothers, please meet with the minister in his study.

This being Easter Sunday, we will ask Mrs. Johnson to come forward and lay an egg on the altar.

The services will close with "Little Drops of Water." One of the ladies will start quietly, and the rest of the congregation will join in.

On Sunday, a special collection will be taken to defray the expenses of the new carpet. All wishing to do something on the new carpet, come forward and get a piece of paper.

The ladies of the church have cast off clothing of every kind and they may be seen in the church basement on Friday afternoon.

A bean supper will be held Saturday evening in the church basement. Music will follow.

The rosebud on the altar this morning is to announce the birth of David Alan Belser, the sin of Rev. and Mrs. Julius Belser.

We will be distributing VBS flies this afternoon.

The ladies are invited to a miscellaneous bridle tea.

As she was preparing to come to church last Sunday, she suffered a small stoke.

Thank you for your sympathy and the lovely pot plant.

The topic for the Elder's Bible class will be "Sinplicity of Christianity."

Next Friday we will be serving hot gods for lunch.

As soon as the weather clears, the men will have a goof outing.

Adult dinner menu: Road beef, potatoes, and gravy.

Half of our difficulty in doing anything worthy of high calling is the shrinking anticipation of its possible after consequences.

Join us in the fellowship room for impromptu adult entertainment.

The nursery is back to the right. The switch is on the wall.

In a bulletin there was an old clothes drive notice that said "No T shits or shorts."

To meet again in that home, where there will be no sorrow, no death, and no rears.

In the classifieds of a church magazine, an ad was inserted about a church looking for a new minister. It said, "Starts August 6, 1991. Send resume by June 1. Include wife, transcripts, and references."
— *Ollie Yeats, OK*

Don't forget, Saturday the ladies in the Secret Sister program will be revealing themselves.

Sermon outline: 1) Delineate your fear, 2) Disown your fear, 3) Display your rear.

"What an incredible story," he said using a lucrative hand gesture.

The Johnson family will attend the funeral of Susie's former husband who died in Detroit, Mich., tomorrow.

The Smiths will be leaving for Texas, where Bill will be attached to the hospital post.

"I have shared your FYI-Fear Your Information-column with him."

Pray for Mrs. Smith. She got a good report and the hole is closing.

Blessed are the poot in spirit, for theirs is the kingdom of heaven.

An omitted "g" in a Lenten worship folder changed the theological slant of the call to worship.
Preacher: "Clothe your ministers with righteousness."
People: "Let us sin with joy!"

Barbara C. remains in the hospital and needs blood donors for more transfusions. She is also having trouble sleeping and requests tapes of Bro. Jack's sermons.
— *L.P. Guthery, AL*

Next week's sermon will be from Bro.... He is a peacher from Florida.

Youth group activities will be gin at 3 p.m.

There will be a pot luck dinner shortly after services today. Be prepared to eat 10-15.

— *Betty Wearden, NE*

Let's all be reminded to check the sick-up date sheet. (Instead of the sick up-date sheet.)

After church services, the youth group will have a rape session. (rap)

— *Karen O'Dell, IL*

This evening's songs will be taken from the Scared Collection Hymnal. (Sacred)

Everyone, please check your meekly (weekly) reminder for duties.

The "Over 60's choir" will be disbanded for the summer with the thanks of the entire church.

Pray daily that the Holy Sprit will bless you.

The used clothing sale will begin at 1 p.m. If things don't sell, there will be a price reduction later in the day. Ladies' skirts would drop at 4 p.m., and men's pants lowered shortly after.

The men's fellowship breakfast will meet Tuesday at 12 sharp.

He that believes in Him shall have ever laughing life.

"Cod be with you."

"Sinday's sermon will be announced later."

Next Thursday there will be tryouts for the choir. They need all the help they can get.

"He was kind, obedient, and genital."

"Be sure to attend the Wednesday Evening Lardies Fellowship."

"By the way, for those of you that have children and don't know it, we have a nursery in the basement of the building."

"The new organ has 29 ranks, and 1800 popes."

Holy Saturday — Easter Vigil — 7:30 PM
Easier Festival Service — 10:30 AM

"Anyone not at the church parking lot by noon will be executed."

"Be sure to attend the church bizarre."

In the words for "God Bless Our Native Land," a mistake appeared in the first line of the second verse. Instead of "For her our prayer shall rise," the words were "For her our payment shall rise."

"LUTHERUN" Everyone thought it was a typo, but it wasn't. It was a run-walk money raiser, sponsored by a Lutheran church. Proceeds were to go to the Lutheran World Hunger Relief.

"The Order of Mating will be used this twentieth Sunday after the Pentecost at Peace in Christ at 9:30 a.m.

The meeting was called to order...the agenda was adopted...the minutes were approved...the financial secretary gave a grief report.

The sentence reporting on a guest preacher for an anniversary service read: "The great preacher for the day was a former pastor."

The so-called "Wicked Bible" (London, 1631) left out the "not" and made the commandment read "Thou shalt commit adultery," for which the publisher was fined 3,000 pounds.

The "Vinegar Bible" (Oxford, 1716-17) substituted "vinegar" for "vineyard" in Luke 22:9.

The "Wife-Hater Bible" (Oxford, 1810) where Luke

13:26 came out "If any man come to Me and hate not... his own wife (life) also, he cannot be My disciple."

Another MARRIAGE ENCOUNTER weekend is being offered. It's a chance for a weekend away for just you and your souse.

Beginning Again Seminar: Help for the Formally Married.

— *Liz Curtis Higgs, KY*

"Whom the Lord loves, he chases."

Song #668 When We Meet In Tweet Communion

Song #663 To Go Be The Glory

On Sunday nights we sometimes had a "Sing-a-long." My bulletin typist omitted one letter in the announcement that left it saying, "7 p.m. tonight, Sin-a-long with Stan."

— *Stan Schrag, NE*

Sermon topic — "The Washing of Hands: Commentary on hind washing."

Hymn #228 — "Jesus Lies, and So Shall I"

This Easter Sunday bulletin caused worshippers to smile. Sunday Sermon: "The Greatest News Ever!" Monday: Pastor's Day Off.

"We hope there will be good attendance for this suspicious occasion."

This particular October events calendar listed: Barker/Renewal of Wedding Vowels.

"Pastor is on vacation, massages can be given to church secretary."

The offertory hymn "Take My Life" was listed as "Table My Life."

"We have an exceptional well-brained pastor."

The closing hymn was listed as, "Jesus, Priceless Pressure."

A congregation with Swedish heritage listed the hymn, "Amazing Grace, How Swede the Sound."

"The Odor of Worship is as follows."

One student may have said more than he meant when he wrote about the Apostles Creed, that he believed in "one holy chaotic church."

One boy spoke of baptism by saying, "Unlike the Baptists who believe in total erosion, we Lutherans believe...."

A newspaper's ad carrying an advance notice about a well-known speaker may have promised too much. It ended with "A brief business meeting and conversion with the speaker is planned."

The announcement for our church picnic was supposed to urge people to arrive in informal clothing. It read, "Everyone is asked to wear clothing for the picnic."

Someone had called the bakery to order a cake inscribed, "Happy Birthday, Pastor Bock." As the chaplain entered the lounge, he was startled to see the frosting read, "Happy Birthday, Pass the Buck."

In our church, to aid in the process of welcoming guests, we have ushers quickly fill out information cards as they seat them. One Sunday, the pastor warmly greeted "Lt. Col. Red Mercedes."
Everyone soon realized that the usher, using certain abbreviations, had been trying to tell the pastor there was a "light-colored red Mercedes" with lights on in the parking lot.

Computer printouts have added bright spots to our church's business meetings. The account description column is limited to relatively few spaces. Last month in approving the purchase of a license, we approved an item which read, "Food Handler's Lice — $600."

Our church newsletter advertised a men's fishing

retreat weekend complete with cabins, boatslips, lake, and lodge for $25.00 a reservation. The date for the weekend was listed as "March 30-June 1."

Our newsletter introduced a new member this way. "I want you to meet Patsy ___, who is a champion swinger."

After being invited over for Sunday lunch, our pastor ended the service with "May the Lord look upon you with flavor and give you peace."

Our new pastor is the Rev. Rebecca Ebb. Our bulletin read, "Please indicate the areas of ministry you could help in and return this form to a member of the committee or Pastor Egg."

A letter which ran in a bulletin explained how the Lutheran Church in America distributes gifts for natural disaster relief. It read, "Natural disasters within the United States are coordinated by the Division for Mission in North America."

Penny ___ begins her internship in the King County Prosecutor's Office this week. Please remember the Prosecutor's Office in your prayers."

"A worm welcome to Kathy ___, our guest organist."

"We welcome the Rev. Howard Kuhnie as our gust speaker."

"We give a haughty welcome to the Rev. LeRoy ___, who will bring us our lesson today."

"If you have not yet received the information, please sue the pastor."

This bulletin announced the fall barbecue with these words, "Bring something for yourself and some-one else to BBQ."

The closing song will be "Prince of Peach, Control my Will."

"Many items have been left in the church during the past several weeks, including hates, gloves, umbrellas, and coats."

The prelude for Sunday, June 21, was listed as POP and CIRCUMSTANCE. Appropriately, that Sunday was Father's Day.

This fund-raising package was addressed to "Holy Gross Lutheran Youth Group" instead of "Holy Cross."

Our secretary must have been thinking of an upcoming event in the King County, Wash., domed stadium when she typed in the Sunday bulletin, "The Kingdome of God."

"LUTHERAN PERISH Worker Wanted."

"The original sin in the new office was too small so a larger one was purchased and installed."

"SELECTION COMMITTEE meets Wednesday, 7 p.m., in the Bride's Room."

"The church women are planning an 'English Tea Party', inviting the women of area Lutheran churches. All women are asked to wear hats and gloves; no slacks please."

"There will not be a covered dish dinner on Dec. 10. Pans have been changed."

"Salvation Army would appreciate receiving canned or boxed groceries, good used sweaters and good used boys for their Christmas assistance program."

"Dec. 9. Christmas Shopping Trip-If you are planning to attend, please sign on your Worship Resister Card."

"Christmas luncheon at the Quality Inn. Lunch at 12:30. Bring an unwrapped gift or man or lady."

"The Service of the Word for Healing, which was cancelled due to pastor's illness, has been rescheduled."

"The Christmas decorating party for church starts Sunday at 2 p.m. Bring your saws to cut trees and willing hands."

"Grace Lutheran Church is looking for a 4-year-old preschool teacher."

"Mid week services are still focusing on the Seven Deadly Sins. This week 'Greed and Gluttony.' Join us for services at 7:30, and come earlier for soup and salad at 6:30."

During the dedication of our new public-address system, one of the congregational responses in the bulletin was, "God bless our sound reproduction facilities!"

"We will be having only one service this summer beginning at 9 a.m. June 5, continuing through Sept. 15."

"Then we are mindful that we always live as recipients of God's underserved love."

OFFERING ANTHEM: "Give It Away."

"Flavorable comments were made concerning the use of a loaf of bread instead of wafers for communion."

"Each Wednesday during Advent, the congregation will gather for prayer, medication, and preparation."

"A prerequisite of choir this year is that you must attend 3/4 of the rehearsals in order to sin."

Our Savior Lutheran Church, recently received an envelope addressed to: "OUR SURVIVOR'S LUTHERAN CHURCH."

As the coffin was lifted and carried to the altar, more than 3,000 mourners sang the hymn, "O God Our Health and Age Has Past."

"Beverages and dessert are furnished by the Boars of Parish Education."

"In order that a pastor of this congregation may be devoted to the duties of the office, an adequate salary shall be provided, pain in semi-monthly or monthly installments."

"Shepherd singles have their regular monthly meeting Monday at 9:30. Come and share a cup of coffee, roll and fellowship with other single ladies."

"Council Report — Due to the length of the Parish Council meeting, very little business was conducted."

Army chapel bulletin: "Those interested in sinning in the Reformation service chorus, join us for rehearsal Thursday evening."

"This Sunday is Food Bank Sunday. Please remember your donations to Interfaith Ministries to help elevate hunger in our community."

"Baptismal bonnets on hand are: 3 girls, 1 boy. There are 4 boys in the process of being made."

"Bishop calls for peach in Nambia."

"Needed (food pantry) items are: canned juices, canned vegetables, fruits, meats, macaroni diapers, shampoo, tea,..."

"KIDS OF THE KINGDOM will be going bowling next Sunday. Cost includes 2 games bowling, shoes, pizza, and pot."

"90% of ELCA churches have one or fewer families."

"I will cling to the old rugged cross/and exchange it some day for a crow."

"Organ recital of Lenten music at the Park Church, with linch following, if you desire."

"Baptismal Hymn: I Was There To Hear Your Boring Cry."

"We would like members to write down their favorite hymns and drip them in the offering plate."

"Men should be freshly shaved for the pictorial directory, except for the bearded variety and those with mustaches."

"Lunch will be served following the burial in the church basement."

"The bouquet of flowers is from their children and they are in the bowl from their 40th wedding anniversary."

"St. John's has been asked to donate the following items to the Junior High Camp...4 dozen homemade cookies or candy bras."

"Sunday we will hold a service...at which we will also install our new and old leadership and deceive new members."

"7:30 a.m. Jr. Choir's trip to Noah's Ark. Rain date is June 27."

"SERMON: 'How to burn without burning out'... Pastor Wick."

"Next Sunday's Forum will deal with the subject of cremation. The guest speaker will be Mike Ashburn."

"March 21, 7:30 p.m. — Worship followed by coffee. 'Weak Yet Strong' Compassion."

"Lenton Service with the St. Jacob players resenting the play, NO NAME STREET."

"Building money will be used for insulting the west wall of the fellowship hall."

"Friday: Church Women United-Retreat at Our Lady of the Mountain."

"We want to sing our favorite hymns this summer. You can help by listing three hums from the hymnal and put your name below."

Our church's Easter breakfast was advertised as "No Resurrection Necessary" to be admitted.

"Holy Communion will be served on the first Sunday, on Maundy Thursday, and on Eater Sunday."

"Let us confess our sin to God...who has promised to forgive and cleanse us from all nutritiousness."

"...your old men shall dream reams, and your young men shall see visions."

"In conjunction with the annual meeting, a lunch persisting of spaghetti and meatballs will be served."

A letter to Rev. John E. Priest said, "Dear Pastor Priest."

"Rachel Circle will resume their meetings on Jan. 27. Call ladies of the church are invited."

"Please greet the newest embers in the Fellowship Hall."

"The men's group will hold their annual meeting. The offering will be taken for the Salvation Army. Bring your wife!"

"God never gives us more than we can bare."

"Saturday activities include special interest groups (self worth, single parent families, the treat of legal gambling, spouse abuse . . .)"

"Pastor Knutson was elected bishop and with him goes the hopes, prayers, and dreams of a synod."

"Thanks to all those who shared all those beautiful Poinsettia pants with the congregation during the holidays."

"An oyster or children dinner is available between 1 and 5:30."

Church camp announcement: "Be a cool dud and come to Camp Shep."

Meeting topic: "Women's rule in the church."

4:30 p.m. — SMORGASBORD
6:30 p.m. — Suicide Survivors Support Group.

GIFTS AND MEMORIALS: $400 for Elevator Fun given by Helen.

"Before the lecture he will be discussing his personal faith struggle in suffering at a potluck dinner."

"Following the meeting they will go out and pick up their section of Hwy 34."

"Singles on the church roof were checked out. We have some on hand and will replace them next spring."

"L.W. will pray for weeds in the parking lot and sidewalks."

"Thanks for sending me the material on the hot for profit housing corporation you are forming."

"Hymn of the day — Give To Our God Immoral Praise."

"People over 60, please visit our Senior Center. Males daily, programs, bus trips year round."

Church Council Minutes Summary, "Exterminator took on the ant problem. One year warranty. Inactive members being contacted."

"The men not only helped set up, but also cooked the children and cleaned up after!"

The 1991 Spring Council Retreat will be hell May 10 and 11.

"A group has been formed to help stagnate churches."

This church sent this notice of its congregational meeting "to decide questions concerning the furnace and the pastoral call."

"7 p.m.: Pre-Martial Workshop and Wedding Service."

The Extension office will present a program on premenstrual syndrome and how it affects women at St. Matthew Lutheran Church.

"Please bring an offering and a snake to share."

"LSS FOOD PANTRY needs food. Michelle __, who runs the pantry, has fun out of money to buy food."

"There will not be a Week of Prayer for United Service next Sunday, due to schedule conflicts for five of the six congregations involved."

"You, as a spiritual leader in Sacramento, are encouraged to attend, be robbed, and participate in the procession."

"Easter Sunrise Service, Sunday, 6 p.m."

Fund raiser for the Benefit Floor breakfast: "So plan now to eat breakfast at the church, make a contribution, and then see your results on the floor."

Treasurer's Report: "We finally took in more for the year than we spent, even with the once-a-year insurance bull of $2,653."

The final Lenten Service theme is: "Why Doesn't God Do Something?" with Pastor Meidinger.

On the church kitchen bulletin board: "Egg Dippers — Make Sure You Cover Your Bottoms!" (Posted after complaints that some of the Easter eggs bottoms weren't covered with chocolate.)

"The correspondence committee will assist with the mailing of the newsletter and stapling of the Annual Report to congregational members."

Musician Wanted: "Must be able to play piano in Spanish for two services."

"Organ recital on Sunday at 3 p.m. Mark your calendar for two services."

"Midnight Mass will begin at 10 p.m.
— *JoAnn Groteluschen, NE*

"Start saving your aluminum cans and bring them to church on Sunday. If you cannot get your cans to church, contact any youth group member to help you."

"The pastor's class for prospective members and other inquirers will meet Sundays in the conference room of the lover level."

"Confirmation classes will be held the second and fourth Sundays of each week."

"Bring potluck dish and drink to share. Hot dogs, hamburgers, and children will be provided as well as paper products."

"What 'ere we do for thin/O Lord, we do it unto thee."

Item for sale: "Used church lights. Contact pastor during the day."

"World Hugger Sunday — Special world hunger offering opportunity."

A local restaurant included on its Sunday menu: "Baked Fillet of Soul."

"Scavenger Hung to help the Food Pantry."

"Moving the church lawn this week will be Allen ___ and Roland ___."

The teacher training workshop promotes the featured speaker as "recognized for expertise ineffective instruction."

"There will be tables on the porch outside the narthex to answer questions and to purchase Bibles."

We will be having a reception after the service. Libby ___ is coordinating persons to bake cakes and kitchenworkers."

Pastor Brent ___, Pianist Jane ___, Greeters the Brown Family, Users Jack and June Smith.
— *Pam McElhaney, CA*

In our church there is an "over 50's" group that calls itself the "Gold Group." In the bulletin it was announced, "The Old Group will have its fellowship Wednesday night."
— *Jim Lundy, NE*

"There will be a vandalism committee meeting Sunday after services."

"With 60 faulty members, it is the largest seminary in the world."

Communion instructions in this church read: "Communicants will receive the host, then dip it into the wind, and return to the pew."

A Palm Sunday bulletin read: "The palm branches will be collected as you leave to be burned."

For the coffee hour, the announcement read, "The Heinz family is furnishing threats this morning."

As our new church was being built, our pastor reassured us in his newsletter that, "The survivors are outside lining up the angels for the new building."

Our social service committee was conducting its quarterly blood pressure clinic, causing someone to put up this sign in front of the church: "Blood pressure taken in rear."

The member who was supposed to be both lector and offering counter became ill, and the pastor left me this note. "Nancy is sick — can't read or count." It made me wonder what kind of sickness was involved.

The ad for a Lutheran College President asked applicants to send curriculum and vitae and the names of "three referees."

Our congregation was planning an adult class for those considering the church for membership. The classes were advertised as primarily for those of other "demoninational" backgrounds.

A synod pastor was hospitalized with a broken kneecap. A typo with the newsletter notice seemed curiously appropriate. It read, "Your remembrances and cars will be appreciated."

My church recently ran this blood-curdling bulletin announcement: "Our picture gallery is being slowly updated by Gary __. Please cooperate when he approaches you to be shot."

"You are invited to greet Bishop Chilstrom at a reception in his honor...and to worship him at Evening Prayer, 5:30 p.m."

Our church's handbook listed projects for each circle. Due to an error, one project called for the repair of "humans" instead of hymnals.

This church has apparently found a way to measure the impact of its sermons. It recently announced "Blood pressure screening before and after the service."

This church listed among items needed for the food pantry, "port and beans."

Members were reluctant to sign up for a physical fitness program when the announcement read, "Exorcise class."

"The Sharing of the Peach."

The history of this church was going to be dramatized in a unique, most unusual way... "Fellowship hour with display of guilts by women of St. Matthias Church."

A lot of research evidently goes into site location

for synod offices. An official memorandum states that the best choice for offices would be at Trinity Church, Tacoma, because it's "located where Lutherans are most dense."

The sermon topic was announced in the bulletin as "Too Much Noise," with "Pastor Bang preaching."

A recent Sunday bulletin included the following acknowledgment for a member who had done some plastering in the church basement: "Thank you Dick ___ who once again has worked hard to clean the pastor off the basement floor."

John 8:32: "And you shall know the truth, and the truth shall make you mad."

Preparation for Lent included the traditional Shrove Tuesday supper. In the monthly church calendar the invitation read: "Shove Dinner with Service."

"Let goods and kindred go, thy moral life also...."

"Ushers will eat latecomers at these points."

"There will be waxers and strippers available for the Men's Club when they do the fellowship hall floor."

The Lutheran men's group will meet at 6 p.m. Steak, mashed potatoes, green beans, bread, and dessert will be served for a nominal feel."

"There will be a congregational meeting after worship service...to approve the budget for 1989. Please plan not to attend."

"We are having a church blood drive. The soup and sandwich lunch is available for those who give blood and their families."

"Craig ___ is working on the plague for piano fund donors."

THE HYMN: "I've Got a Robe, You've Got a Rob."

"Come and celebrate! Pastor Steve will present his last sermon on Sunday."

FOOD PANTY PROGRAM meets emergency food needs for 6-10 families per week.

"Our sanctuary is now air-conditioned for the summer months and is cooking our summer worshippers."

Our best wishes are extended to Gene and Joan who were yesterday untied in Christian marriage."

In an Army base church bulletin: "Jesus Jeep Me Near the Cross."

"Ricky, Rachael, and Norma are workers on the bus ministry. On Sunday morning they can be seen busy at work in the Fellowship Building mixing and pouring drinks for the Sunday school children."

"Yes, I would like to sin with the choir June 12."

"Do This in Remembrance of Me" is the title of…a special memorial ceremony for members who have died during the past two years at both services."

While welcoming guests and visitors to Sunday morning worship, our bulletin that should have said how "tickled" we were for their presence, read: "We're really ticked that you are here."
— *Dawn Corbin, PA*

"The senior choir invites any member of the congregation who enjoys sinning to join the choir."

"Please join us as we show our support for Amy and Alan in preparing for the girth of their first child."

"Surely He Has Borne Our Briefs."

"The Tired Sunday in Advent."

"Remember in prayer the many who are sick of our community."

Hymn: "In Christ There Is No East."

"The carolers will leave after the evening Advent vesper at 5:30 p.m. and return to the church by 7 for ever delicious chili, which is created by the combining of child from every person."

"If you received a Christmas fruit basket from Augustana, if possible, return it to the church by next November.

"Spend one Sunday each week at your nearest church."

"Please do not immerse the coffee servers."

"Let me be thin forever."

"A nursery is provided at all services, and interpretation for the hearing available at the 10:00 service."

A church project announcement said, "A trailer from Don ___ will be sued for gleaning potatoes as needed."

"BALONY CLASS" The Balcony Sunday school class is beginning a new unit of study.

I sent out 200 photocopied letters to "men of the cloth" seeking their "Bloopers." In this letter I put a cute phrase that said, "To err is human — To share the error is devine." One pastor circled the "de" in devine and sent the letter back to me. It's spelled "di" vine.

Yes, I can laugh at myself.

— *Ken Alley, NE*

"Our Witness Commission is sponsoring a dull-color church directory to help us match names to faces."

"SOMETHING TO GIVE THANKS FOR: Both Les and Rachael were involved in very serious accidents in which the vehicles they were riding were totally destroyed. Thanks be to God."

"The evening service was assigned for those with hearing impairments, and liturgical dancers stimulated the senses in yet another way."

"The first month's men's breakfast was held Saturday and was a huge success. Those present missed a lot!"

"The prayers of the church are asked for Mary, Caroline, and Jacob, who are in need of God's helling grace."

"There will be plenty of room in the oven for those people who bring a hot dish to the church service before the dinner."

"Any monies not raised through the sale of the Organ Certificates will be borrowed eternally."

"Children will be given sermon-related bulleting by the ushers for the use during worship service.

"Fiends at Zion wish you God's blessings at this happy time."

"Eight new black choir robes are currently needed, due to the addition of several new members and to the deterioration of some older ones."

"This church will dedicate four works of art in memory of eight persons who have died over the past several years at the conclusion of the 9:30 worship service Sunday."

"Scouts are saving aluminum cans, bottles and other items to be recycled. Proceeds will be used to cripple children."

"First communion classes will begin on Sunday at 9:45....If interested, please Pastor Wittcopp."

This letter to the church concluded, "Gold bless your thoughts and actions."

"Perhaps envelopes need to be stuffed with senior volunteers for a congregational mailing."

"Lent provides addictional opportunities for worship and prayer."

"The youth are selling delicious frozen pies to raise funds for their Dallas trip. You may see them after services today, or expect a call from one."

"...he filed charges for inappropriate sexual misconduct." (vs. appropriate?)

About 50 years ago in my previous parish, I had to type stencils and print the bulletins because I didn't have a secretary. I had a young lady by the name of Daisy, quite active in the parish, who would help me from time to time. She was quite well proportioned above the hips and below the shoulders.

While thanking her in the bulletin, instead of typing "Daisy", my non-professional script read, "DAIRY." I never did live that one down.

— *Charles Naugle, PA*

This bulletin read, "Ladies of the Evening" Circle will meet at 7:30 tonight.

I didn't really know what to think because I was a visitor to this church. As I kept reading, though, it became more apparent. It was just differentiating this group from the Morning and Afternoon Circles.

— *April Larson, LA*

Weight Watchers will meet at 7 p.m. at the First Presbyterian Church. Please use the large double door at the side entrance.

Housing Needed. We are seeking volunteers to host members of the Clare College Choir for the evening of Monday, September 13th. If you have some extra room and would like to hose two or three of

these college age students from Cambridge, England,
please call Sue.

— Bill Bottorf, NE

While I lay wrapped in sleep and unconscious of
myself, Your sleepless eye kept virgil.

HEY, SEND ME YOUR STORIES!

Chapter 4

Miscellaneous Bloopers

My father, a retired pastor, was visiting from out of state. He was having such a "grandfatherly" time with my little ones, playing catch, reading them stories, tucking them in bed, etc. We were all really glad to see him. On Sunday we went to church and he was asked to lead the congregation in The Lord's Prayer, which he graciously accepted. He arose to the pulpit and asked all to bow their heads and join him in this prayer. He started off, "Now I lay me down to sleep, I pray the Lord my soul to keep...." Everyone laughed, but understood his absentmindedness.

— *Gary Groteluschen, NE*

My first two years of college were spent at a local Christian school. One of the requirements was that you take a Bible class every semester. I was still living at home and regularly attended church where my dad was the minister. I thought I would kill two birds with one stone by doing my college Bible assignments during church. This worked pretty well until one Sunday afternoon Dad asked me what I was doing during the service, since he had noticed my head was bowed throughout the sermon. I told him, and he thought a moment, then said, "Well, don't you think you should be listening to the sermon?" I'll bet that was the only time since Adam met Eve that someone got into trouble for studying the Bible in church.

— *Bob Peters, TX*

I went to visit a parishioner in the hospital. I had forgotten what she was being treated for, and as I came into her room, I noticed she was napping. I took her by the toe and wiggled it, saying, "Wake up, sleepy head." She let out a blood curdling scream. Oh, yeah. She had toe surgery. OOPS!

— *Robert Donner, SC*

My grandmother has a tendency to drop off to sleep during sermons. She does it enough that there is an unwritten family rule that anyone observing this is to give a gentle nudge to wake her up. This is usually done quickly because Grandma will snore if left in her slumber too long. One Sunday, immediately after her third nudge, Grandma stood up right in the middle of the sermon. She must have been confused in her sleep and thought it was time to go home. It was so funny because only she and the Priest were on their feet. Grandma sat down after a few seconds, but the whole pew was rolling with laughter by then.

— *Andy Armstrong, OH*

In my preacher's opening remarks last Sunday, he said that every day is a new day. "We all make decisions from the moment we get up. We decide whether to have breakfast or not. We decide what shoes to wear. We decide whether to wear pants or a skirt...well, women can decide that anyway...because most men don't wear skirts...at least those who belong to this church...I hope. I probably should continue...with my sermon...before I get in more trouble."

— *Don Miller, AZ*

Bumper sticker:
You're in good hands with Allstate.
You're in good hands with Jesus.

The main reason most people go to the church they do is not because they have searched the Scriptures and determined that their church is the right one; but because that's the church they were raised in, the church their parents were raised in, and grandparents, etc. If you would have grown up in another church, you would likely be going there now and wondering why everybody didn't go there.

— *Sandy Batterton, WA*

My preacher told a hilarious story one Sunday about how we do stupid things sometimes and end up paying the price. He compared it to something he did as a child when he and his buddies went out to an empty grain bin. He looked in the doorway and noticed dozens of pigeons roosting inside. He told his friends to watch the pigeons fly when he scared them. He climbed inside the bin and screamed at the top of his lungs, causing a flurry of pigeon activity. He paused in his sermon for a moment and said, "Do you have any idea what a hundred pigeons do when they're scared?"

— Ken Alley, NE

After our regular collection at church, there is often a special collection that we take for any number of things. Ideally the pastor announces the need for a special collection immediately after the regular collection when people will still have their checkbooks out. These extra collections got to be so frequent that one of the ushers suggested it would be easier to announce when there wouldn't be a special collection.

— Randy Sinder, TX

At a prison church service, one visiting church lady asked the inmates if they ever got congregational visits with their spouses. (Conjugal)

I've got a friend who always takes off his shoes during a sermon . . . except when I'm sitting behind him, because I'll reach under the pew and take them and not give them back until we're outside.

— Bobby Taylor, IA

Why don't people tear out their offering checks BEFORE church, instead of making so much noise IN church?

If you want to put a spark into church, as you squeeze by someone sitting on the pew, sit down in their lap for a moment. It's extra fun if that person is a visitor.

One preacher said, "Go fart...I mean, go forth and preach the word."

What we need is to get back to non-skid religion. (Screeeeeeeech!)

One church bulletin said that Jesus was crucified at Cavalry (Charge!) instead of Calvary.

My wife called me at the office as I was typing the above sentence and I asked her how to spell Calvary. She answered, "What are you doing now, re-writing the Bible?" (I will if I want to; there shouldn't be any copyright problems.)

— *Ken Alley, NE*
(The Author)

They are called the Ten COMMANDMENTS, not Ten SUGGESTIONS!

While dressing after an adult baptism, someone opened the dressing room curtain and exposed the back side of the convert to the congregation.

— *Harold Mitchell, NE*

As they reached under the Lord's Table for the collection plates, two ushers knocked heads pretty hard. One fell back and had to be helped back up by the other ushers.

— Bob Stanley, AR

After the adult Bible class was over, everyone quietly snuck out of the room and left my husband, who was sleeping, to wake up on his own.

— Karen Luebbe, OR

A mother's prayer for her child: "Thank God he's in bed."

— Ruth Parks, IL

A sign in front of a church: We're going to heaven some day. If you need a ride, give us a call."

— Willie Tucker, TX

Sign seen in church yard: "When it comes to giving, some people will stop at nothing."

— Bradley Swick, CA

I heard of a church having a "Holy Hole in One" golf tournament.

— Monte Nieman, CA

On hearing that my wife and I recently observed our 50th anniversary, our pastor asked, "How's the second honeymoon going Jack?" I answered, "For your information Monsignor, a second honeymoon can easily be more like a Second World War."

— *Jack Jewell, MA*

I was in a Bible class with a self-proclaimed Biblical genius. He got caught not knowing as much as he let on, and said, "I know all about that, but I've been sworn to secrecy." Is that a blooper?

— *William Tonniges, ND*

I left the door open at the local cafe and one crony said, "Were you born in a barn?" I said, "Yes, me and Jesus."

— *Rodney Maier, TN*

When baptizing by immersion, how long do you leave them under the water? I said, "Long enough to do them some good."

— *Wayne Daneks, WA*

In the middle of a mass, a dog trotted down the center aisle and stopped in front of the altar. The priest paused, looked down at the dog and said, "I don't remember hearing your confession."

— *Barb Skaden, NE*

This question was asked of a missionary, "Do you think in France?" What he meant was, "Do you think in French?"

— *Marilyn Hansen, FL*

One guy ended his prayer with "Yours truly," instead of "In the name of Jesus."

— *Kenny Thonen, WA*

"Praise the Laaard!" (southern drawl)

— *Flo Reinmiller, LA*

Used to answering the company phone, the man opened his prayer, "Sawyer Tractor Company," instead of "Dear God."

— *John Hamm, KS*

While praying for the communion, the "fruit of the vine," was referred to as "fruit of the loom."

— *Robert Ahrens, ID*

Asked about what church he attended, the man said, "I belong to the Faith of the Inner Springs Church." (He slept in on Sundays).

— *Todd Baker, MS*

A sign in front of a church under construction read: "Danger, Men Working Above." I thought to myself, "Isn't that the truth, when men try to take the place of God."

— *Shirley Carpenter, NE*

I knew a pastor whose name was Robert Sinner, and his wife's maiden name was Betty Amen.

— *Kathy Beatty, NY*

I saw a man track down an annoying wasp and smash it between two sections of a song book, is that a blooper? It woke a few people up.

— *Morace Becker, CA*

Keeping a sermon interesting should be a priority for preachers because of people falling asleep during the sermon. One man fell asleep, his head slipped off his hand and hit the pew in front of him, knocked him unconscious and he had to be carried out.

— *Tim Andrews, NJ*

On the way out of a prison service, one well meaning church lady said, "Come and visit us any time," as if they could.

— *Jeanne Chapman, NE*

Asked to interpret the Latin words under The Last Supper Picture, he said "All you fellers that want your picture took, get behind the table."

— *Burt Edgerley, NE*

The name of the religion page editor of this newspaper was Tony Sin.

— *Doyle Anderson, ID*

I was listening to a friend reading the selected scripture before the sermon and instead of saying, "the flaming brazier," he said, "flaming brassiere."

— *Frank Harre, NE*

While baptizing a baby, a cat that had snuck in the church rubbed up against the pastor's leg, causing quite a chuckle.

— *Lydia Romanowski, NE*

While kneeling down on the kneeler bench, the pastor lost his balance and continued over and fell on his face.

— *Lydia Romanowski, NE*

I hate it when the song director introduces a new song at the end of a service. "There's a time for new songs and it's not at the end of a service," I thought as I hummed it all the way home.

— *Loren Anderson, NM*

There was this man who always slept in church. When he was awakened, he would say "Amen," as if he was in silent prayer.

— *Owen Bailey, MN*

Tennis in the Bible: When Moses served in Pharoah's court.
Baseball in the Bible: In the Big Inning.
The Bible in football: The Immaculate Reception.

— *Sue Curran, NE*

The only mention of a car in the Bible: The disciples were in one "accord." (Honda?)

— *Karen Palik, NE*

During the spring of each year, given the conditions are right, the sun reflects off a stained glass window and hits the preacher right between the eyes. It's happened enough times that he has become paranoid about springtime.

— Sharon Hubbard, ID

God's first name is Andy. Andy walks with me, Andy talks with me, Andy tells me I am his own.

— Karen Palik, NE

Two true friends were in a church choir performance. One of them became ill and thought he should quietly exit over the back of the bleachers. As he was excusing himself, the other friend had hold of his robe and wouldn't let go until the last tug. The sick one lost his balance and crashed his hard soled shoes on the hard floor, creating quite a ruckus!

— Steve Ferguson, NE

The song was announced "Amaze me Grace," instead of "Amazing Grace."

— Eugene Irmer, MN

On sharing a common communion cup, one gal said, "I believe in God, but I don't think he'll keep me from catching the flu."

— Joan Piesinger, AZ

Hurrying to church was always a Sunday habit for this family. Finally, settling down, thinking peace had come, their little three-year-old daughter stood up on the seat, grabbed the back of the pew in front of her, and leaned way forward. Low and behold, in their rush to get to church on time, they had forgotten to put panties on her. Half of the audience saw the sweetest little bottom God ever made.

— *Linda Sackschewsky, NE*

In the middle of his sermon the preacher's wife fell asleep. Her head nodded back and her mouth opened up wide, causing her jaws to lock. The preacher had to stop what he was doing to help his wife shut her mouth.

— *Sara Monson, FL*

One man's reason for never shoveling the snow, "The Lord giveth, the Lord taketh away."

— *Elmer Barrett, NE*

Sneaking a transistor radio into a service and listening in on a ball game through an ear phone can cause some interruption. As a home run was hit, a seemingly attentive man hollers out, "Yeah, Baby!" instead of "Praise the Lord."

— *Kevin Walbrecht, TN*

The preacher was making his final point in his sermon, but had a ways to go. The song leader hopped right in and lead the invitation song before the preacher was through.

— *Al Kenly, WA*

I was in a service once where the song director pitched a song way too high, and stopped to re-pitch it, only to start over at the same pitch the second time.

— *Deanna Wats, MN*

My daughter asked me why there was a cross spray painted on her aunt's back window screen of her house. Auntie was a very bad housekeeper and I didn't want to put her down in front of my daughter, so I told her I didn't know, but secretly I figured the cross was the only thing keeping the demons out.

— *Al Kenly, WA*

One summer day there were three nuns doing some remodeling at the church building. It was so hot that one of the nuns said, "You know, if we lock the doors and shut the stained glass windows, we could do this work in our underwear." They decided to do that, and found that it was much more comfortable.

In about an hour there was a knock on the front door. This startled the nuns a little bit and one of them asked, "Who is it?" "It's the blind man," came the answer. One nun said to let him in because he couldn't see anything. So they did, and as the blind man came into the foyer, he said, "Hey, nice undies, where do you want these blinds?"

— *(Joke)*

This Pentecost Cake was to read "Let the Spirit in." When it was delivered to the church, it read "Let the Spirit End."

— *Donald Cellar, MI*

At a ball game, a fellow church member asked if I knew where the pastor was. I didn't, but my young son jumped in and said, "I just saw him down by the confession stand."

— *Pat Thompson, AZ*

As our adult class was studying about Jonah my husband said, "I don't think I can stomach that."

— *Nadine Bunker, VA*

Not knowing what budget category to put a recent purchase of "Pampers" in, the church secretary finally decided on "Youth Activities."

— *Greg Dunsse, FL*

As I took off my coat in the foyer, I was embarrassed to find myself adorned in a full slip and pull over apron. In my hurry to get everyone ready for church, I had forgotten to dress myself.

— *Olga Peterson, AR*

One Sunday morning after the sermon, a lady responded to the invitation song and came forward to seek the grace of Jesus. It was customary for the responding member to fill out a card to let the preacher know why she had come, and what she needed in the way of the church.

The preacher noticed this lady looked somewhat puzzled by some aspect of the card, so he went over to help her. He found that he had given her, by mistake, a Christian Camp Enrollment Card. The lady, who had come forward to be baptized, was puzzled by the first question on the form following the name and address: "Can you swim?"

— (Joke)

Two senior pastors were arguing about the subject of sex relations in marriage. One said sex was 40% fun and 60% work, and the other said sex was 60% fun and 40% work. The youth minister was eaves-dropping and said, "Well, I think it must be 100% fun, because if there was any work to it, you two would make me do it!"

— (Joke)

Famous toast, "May we all be in heaven 30 minutes before the devil knows we're dead."

— Joseph Zieg, KS

A preacher was telling a parent about his son's swearing and how it interrupted his class. The dad said, "I don't know where that blankety-blank kid gets that stuff!"

— Leslie White, TX

I was directing a song before the sermon and asked the congregation to only sing the first two verses, and after the sermon, sing the last two. After we finished the first two verses, four people continued and finished the entire song by themselves.

— Al Kenly, WA

I think priests should be allowed to marry. Let them find out what Hell is really like!

— *Bob Wilson, TN*

I asked a man, "Hey, did you get anything out of my sermon?" He answered, "Yes, a nap!"

— *Gerald Anderson, KY*

Whoever was supposed to say the closing prayer wasn't around to do it, so eventually two different men got up from different sides of the building to fill in. They unexpectedly met on the stage, and then both decided to let the other one say the prayer, and both turned around to go back. Neither one knew what to do until the preacher finally pointed his finger to one of them.

— *Andrew Zimmerman, CA*

During a silent prayer, one of the ushers started snoring, and the priest had to wake him up.

— *Mary Kay Wray, NY*

An old Indian's estimate of a preacher noted for loud, but useless preaching, "Big wind, great thunder, but no rain."

— *LaVerne Hoyle, AZ*

One member of the church financial committee thanked a wealthy Texan for his generous contribution. The Texan said, "Just had my first gusher come in, and thought I'd catch up on my giving."

— *Bruce Hoffman, TX*

THE LESSON

Then Jesus took his disciples up the mountain, gathered them around him, and taught them saying:

Blessed are the poor in spirit, for theirs is the kingdom of heaven.

Blessed are the meek, blessed are they that mourn, blessed are the merciful, blessed are they who thirst for justice, blessed are you when you suffer. Be glad and rejoice, for your reward is great in heaven.

Then Simon Peter said, "Do we have to write this down?"

Then Andrew said, "Are we supposed to know this?"

Then James said, "Will this be on the test?"

Phillip said, "I don't have any paper."

Bartholemew said, "Do we have to turn this in?"

And John said, "The other Disciples didn't have to learn this."

And Matthew said, "Can I go to the bathroom?"

And Judas said, "When will we use this in real life?"

Then one of the Pharisees who was present asked to see Jesus's lesson plan and inquired of Jesus, "Where is your anticipatory set of objectives in the cognitive domain?"

. . . . And Jesus wept . . . .

— *Author unknown*

At the end of a marriage counseling session, the wife was putting on her coat and she asked her husband if it made her look fat. He said, "No, but your rear end does." I asked her to wait in the car while I had another talk with her husband.

— Jacob Lloyd, NE

I heard a woman ask the preacher's wife after a Sunday service, "What do you do with him the rest of the week?"

— Diane Harre, MI

After a sermon, one guy said to me, "That one really put me to sleep."

— Dennis Weiss, MT

The portable choir bleachers were set up right in front of the baptistry. During a practice session, one of the guys on the top row pulled a guy's hair on the second row one too many times. You can guess the rest! (Kerr-splash!)

— Al Kenly, WA

After driving by the church and seeing a combine in the parking lot, my husband remarked that the Elders must be separating the wheat from the chaff today.

— Betty Ferguson, KS

The opening scripture was Psalms 81:10, "Open your mouth wide, and I will fill it."

I thought it funny that the man who read it was a local dentist!

— Dale Goesch, OR

Biblical reason for the husband to help around the kitchen: II Kings 21:13, "I will wipe Jerusalem as a man wipeth a dish, wiping it and turning it upside down."

— *Paula Larson, OK*

A lady, judging a poster contest at St. Joe Elementary School, thought the only fair way was to go, "Eenie, Meenie, Miney, Mo, catch a Catholic by the toe."

— *Jan Speidle, CA*

I overheard my doctor husband answer a question from one of our kids, "What's that thing around the pastor's neck?" He said, "That's called a cervical collar." I gently corrected him, "It's referred to as a clerical collar, Dear."

— *Jane Kenly, WA*

On the outside sign board, the next Sunday's sermon was announced. "We have no wine." By the next Saturday, on top of the board was a bottle of Chablis.

— *Julie Steirs, AZ*

I heard of a church bowling team called the "Holy Rollers."

— *Tracy Stett, MN*

I remember a man telling the story of how he prayed and prayed for a son. Upon the delivery of twins, he wondered if he had prayed too much.

— *Richard Stephens, MO*

The church sign board read:

Sunday morning sermon: "Jesus Walking on Water."

Sunday evening sermon: "Looking for Jesus."

—Wayne Keller, WA

During a solemn mass, I sneezed and my hat sailed off my head, landing two pews forward. Everyone behind me got a chuckle out of that.

— Marion Demange, IL

As a young child continued to wail between his two parents, the husband whispered to the wife in measured tones, "WHY-DON'T-YOU-TAKE-HIM-OUT?" Her soft but deliberate reply was, "I-DON'T-WANT-TO-CREATE-A-SCENE!"

— Marion Demange, IL

The song director was going to have different sections of the congregation sing a short chant. He said, "This will be sung in intervals like the 'Row, Row, Row Your Boat' round," to be sure all knew what he meant. As he started the first group off he sang, "Row, row, row your boat," by mistake. He decided he blew it, and went on to the next song.

— Al Kenly, WA

During a sermon on giving, the preacher heard a grown man laugh out loud, not exactly the kind of response one would expect with this topic. The guilty man apologized after the service and said that Satan was tempting him to not give any money this week because he would need it tonight at the bowling alley. He almost gave in but decided he would keep the cash for later but write out a check for twice his usual contribution so Satan wouldn't bother him again.

— *Gene Bartles, AZ*

I heard of a time when the choir was walking in and one of the girls got her heel stuck in a heat grate. The boy behind her bent over to pull her heel out but as he lifted the shoe up the entire grate came with it. His momentum carried him forward, and the boy behind him, thinking all was well, took a step forward and ended up in the hole.

— *Julie Stenson, AZ*

I wore a skirt to church that fastened with snaps. We stood as the pastor gave the benediction, and low and behold, my skirt dropped to the floor. It must have come undone while I was sitting and I didn't realize it. No one laughed then, but I'm sure they did on their way home.

— *Lorna Wiens, NE*

I overheard a lady remark about how bad her back hurt after sitting on those hard pews. Her friend said she thought God should take care of something like that during services.

— *Al Kenly, WA*

I was following a lady out of services one day and watched her walk right out of her slip. Come to find out, the embarrassed lady had forgotten to put her arms through the straps of her slip and so there wasn't anything holding it up.

— *Bettye Jo Hamm, KS*

After singing the closing hymn, a visitor in front of me turned and said on his way out, "Don't give up your day job."

— *Rupert Speece, NY*

I was observing an adult immersion baptism when I noticed the preacher's underwear showing through his white baptismal clothing after it had become wet. After the service, the preacher's wife was telling everyone that all he had to wear that morning was his Valentine's Day underwear, which happened to have big red hearts all over it!

— *Alice Thayer, NE*

A sign on the pastor's door said, "Have flu, be back tomorrow GLW." I finally had to ask the pastor what GLW meant because it wasn't his initials, and he said, "Good Lord willing." I should have known that.

— *Joe Simon, NH*

A man reading the announcements read, "Husband has gone to see wife, desires prayers" instead of "Husband has gone to sea, wife desires prayers."

— *Dale Grim, NE*

In a heated Bible class discussion, a comment was made about "not giving a rat's ass" about something.

— *Mike Sherman, NC*

My all-time favorite sermon was titled, "THE LESS YOU SAY, THE LESS YOU HAVE TO TAKE BACK." Good material, and the preacher said it all in 15 minutes.

— *Mark Stevenson, KY*

I've noticed the people who come late for services, sleep through my sermons, and complain about everything, are the same ones who back their cars into their parking stalls, ready for a quick get-away as soon as services are over.

— *Al Kenly, WA*

We were comparing different churches and one guy said, "We all work for the same boss, just different stores."

— *Pauline Shockey, MO*

I was listening to a sermon that compared the good and the bad that can happen in one's life, when the preacher referred to America as the "Sweet Land of Misery," instead of "Sweet Land of Liberty."

— *William Stanton, TN*

Bumper Stickers seen in church parking lots:
> If you are going the wrong direction, God allows U-turns.

God is alive.

No Jesus . . . No Peace
Know Jesus . . . Know Peace

God is my co-pilot.

God is real.

Christians aren't perfect . . . just forgiven.

My boss is a Jewish Carpenter.

Live so the preacher won't have to lie at your funeral.

I owe, I owe . . . It's off to church I go.

Seven days without Christian fellowship makes one
   "weak."

I'd rather be fishing.

During the sermon, the preacher made several statements, hoping for some "AMENS." He finally got one when he said "and in conclusion."
                              — *Eldon Snider, MA*

I overheard a mechanic say he had to go out and replace a "Jesus Pin" on a John Deere combine. Stumped as to what he meant, I asked him to define "Jesus Pin" for me. He said it was an itty bitty pin that's way up under the crank shaft, and it's extremely hard to get to, take out, and replace . . . and it always made him say "Jeeeeeeeesus!" when he had to work on one.

I couldn't tell if he was swearing or praying.

— *Bob Stair, AZ*

One evening at church, all the flowers that were used at the wedding earlier were placed by the pulpit. In the middle of the sermon, a bumble bee came out from one of the flower displays and caused the preacher to lose his train of thought for quite some time.

— *Arthur Schuessler, MI*

I was part of a gospel singing group that did lots of traveling. At the end of one performance, one of our group was to sing a solo, and we were all supposed to exit behind the stage and go down the stairs to the basement that led back to the front of the church.

When the singer finished, we started our exit to the left; but the lone soloist went to the right and entered another door, which happened to be a big broom closet. Not knowing what to do, he lingered for a moment, but then decided to come out and face the embarrassment. The closing prayer didn't have much effect because most of the congregation had big smiles on their faces.

— *Dave Kats, NE*

Someone at our church got real serious about replacing the pews with 250 recliners.

— *Rich Schoch, OR*

My arthritis doctor told me he didn't want me on my knees unless I heard the Lord was coming.

— *Merna Jacobson, SC*

As I was driving down the highway, I passed "Anderson Cemetery." I thought to myself, "Who would want a cemetery named after them?" Let's see…"Alley Cemetery…nope, doesn't do a thing for me."

— *Ken Alley, NE*

A "Sunday only" sign at a car dealer said, "We will not be undersouled."

— *Dave Schramn, IA*

The song leader stood up and began to lead the hymn "Holy, Holy, Holy." Unfortunately, he started the hymn an octave too high, and sang "Holy, Holy, Holy, Lord God all mighty…that's too high!"

— *Jeff Jaros, MD*

I got up to the podium to read the selected scripture and said, "Would you please turn to Philations 3:15." Normally it takes just a few moments for the congregation to thumb to it in their Bibles, but for some reason they all just sat there.

I thought maybe they hadn't understood me so I repeated myself, "Philations 3:15." Still, nobody moved. Someone in the front row asked, "Did you mean Philippians or Galations?"

Most got quite a kick out of my "Blooper" because they knew I was writing this book.

— *Ken Alley, NE*

Our song director, who was also reading the scripture before the sermon said, "Would you please turn your hymnals to Matthew:5.

— Sandy Hoeman, WV

As I was listening to our pastor speak on the subject of adultery, a helium filled balloon, which escaped from the youth group's party the night before, started settling behind the pastor. The smiley face on the balloon was just a little inappropriate for the sermon topic.

— May Townsen, AR

We have a song director that also has a radio show on the local station. One Sunday he said, "The prayer after this song will be brought to you by Jerry Simon…of Simon Auto Sales."

— Barry Jones, ND

On the marquee in front of the local theater, the movie was advertised, "U FORGIVEN." (with Clint Eastwood) The N had fallen down.

— Ken Alley, NE

WAYS TO AVOID CHURCH
1. On Saturday night poll your children as to their availability on Sunday morning, then put church attendance to a vote.
2. Plan a late Saturday night with the potential for a good Sunday morning headache.
3. Be sure there is either no gas in the car or the battery is dead.

4. Plan an elaborate Sunday breakfast to ensure that following it there will be no time to dress.
5. At dinner on Saturday discuss those things which bother you about the church and its clergy.
6. In the name of "family togetherness" plan your own three minute Sunday service at home.
7. Make sure that your family is signed up for all Sunday morning "sports opportunities."
8. On Sunday morning "discover" that an important report must be completed before Monday's office arrival.
9. If all else fails, drive your children to church, drop them off, and seek solace in a cup of coffee and The New York Times while you wait for your children to "get religion."
10. Rectors are not supposed to have a sense of humor; boycott those who do.

— Rev. Walter H. Taylor, Rector
Reprinted with permission
— ANGLICAN DIGEST

NINE COMMANDMENTS FOR ALTAR GUILDS

If it's metal, polish it.
If it's floral, arrange it.
If it's cloth, iron it.
If in doubt, wash it.
If it's been taken care of by one person for more than ten years, avoid it.
If it's a memorial, revere it or try to work around it.

If it's been done only one way for more than five
years, don't try to change it.
If new rectors, vicars, or curates get bright ideas,
indulge them. They'll soon learn better.
If the bishop wants all the vestments and hangings
changed ten minutes before the service, smile
sweetly, ask him to pray for a speedy recovery
from your hearing loss, and leave him to his
prayers in the solitude of the sacristy.

— *via St. Mary's Church, Madisonvilly, KY*
Reprinted with permission
— *ANGLICAN DIGEST.*

EXCUSES WHY PEOPLE DON'T GO TO CHURCH

It's easier to watch what's-his-name on TV.
We went last week.
I knew the pastor in college.
My ex-wife goes there.
My ex-husband goes there.
I haven't sinned much lately.
It makes lunch late.
I can't stand crying babies.
Sitting on pews hurts my hemorrhoids.
The bridge was out.
Turning the song book pages makes my fingers
tired.
We didn't want to walk in late, so we didn't go at all.
It exhausts me.
It's none of your business. What are you doing,
writing a book?

A local fire inspector, who happened to be Lutheran, walked into a local Church of Christ to do its required inspection. As he wandered around, he walked into a dark room and promptly fell into a filled baptistry.

Now people tease him about getting immersed just in case sprinkling ends up not being scriptural on judgment day.

— *Helen Amberg, IN*

An elderly gentleman was going to dismiss us with a prayer and he said, "Will you reverently stand on your heads and bow your feet." It really cracked me up.

— *Carol Shafer, NE*

FOOTBALL CHRISTIANITY

Quarterback Sneak: Communicants who quietly exit immediately following communion, a quarter of the way through the service or near the last quarter of the service.

Draft Choice: Selection of a seat near the door.

Draw Play: What many children (and a few adults) do with their service leaflets.

Halftime: The time between the peace and offertory.

Benchwarmer: Those whose only participation is their attendance on Sunday morning.

Fumble: Dropping a hymnal, singing the wrong verse, and general inattention to the prayer book.

Backfield in Motion: Making two or three trips out of the church during the sermon.

Stay in the Pocket: What happens to a lot of money that should go toward missions.

Two-Minute Warning: When the rector begins cleansing the vessels after communion, giving everyone time to shuffle prayer books and hymnals, and gather belongings.

Sudden Death: The rector going overtime.

Blitz: The stampede for the doors after services.

Halfback Option: When 50% of the congregation does not return for Evensong.

> — *The Anglican Digest*
> *Reprinted with permission 10-28-92.*

When our son was three, we lived an hour's drive from church. Since he often napped on the way home, we allowed him to take his bedtime blanket (which had been reduced to nothing more than a rag). He was supposed to leave it in the car, though, while we were in church.

Sunday after Sunday he would start fussing as the

sermon began, wanting his blanket. We would quietly argue with him, telling him he was too big to be dragging it into church. There were times we missed half the sermon because of him wanting his blanket.

One hot, summer Sunday, I reached the end of my rope and took him out of church to the parking lot. I scolded him, swatted him and put him in his car seat with his ratty blanket, telling him that if he wanted his blanket, he would have to stay in the car and would not be allowed in church.

I then went to stand in the back of the church where I could listen to the sermon and still watch him through the open door. I had to leave the windows of the car down, of course, because of the heat. It wasn't long before he started wailing like I had beat him. When church ended, all the elderly members walked right past me without saying a word, out to our car, and made over my son as if he was the most abused child in the world.

Did I ever feel like a cruel mother!!

— *Judi Domeier, NE*

While counseling a transient member on job opportunities, I asked him if he had any money. He said he was flat broke. "Not even have $100 tucked away somewhere?" I asked. He said, "If I had $100, I wouldn't need a job."

— *Jim Anderson, MN*

While baptizing a child 36 years ago, a little feather detached from a pigeon flying outside and blew through an open window. It landed on the baptismal font, quite symbolic of the Baptism of Christ when the Holy Spirit descended on him like a dove. The family still has the feather.

— *Charles Naugle, PA*

Before introducing the guest speaker, the song director nodded a "thank you" to the organist (a very buxomous woman). He then proceeded to introduce Pastor "Boob" Alexander from Dallas."

— *Al Brumbaugh, TX*

Two notices side by side on the bulletin board:
Pastor Bob is on vacation.
Praise the Lord!

— *Milo Deken, KS*

A woman evangelist, about 6'3", was known for her long prayers when approaching the Lord about the needs of the congregation. She would go on and on and on with general pleas to the point where many people would just quit praying and open their eyes, look around and entertain themselves.

One prayer, as she finally approached the specific needs of individuals, she said, "And now Lord, we beseech thee for those that really need help." Her husband, a 5'5" baker, raised his hand for everybody to see and pointed to her.

— *Dean Daniels, MO*

We were singing "All Hail the Power of Jesus' Name" when I overheard the man behind me sing, "Let angels prostate fall."

— *Rita Morrow, LA*

Out of respect for a dear, 100 year old lady, the congregation sang "Happy Birthday" to her. After everyone applauded, the song director said that we were dismissed. He stopped, looked stupid, and asked one of the Elders if it was scriptural to close a service with the singing of Happy Birthday. Since half the people were already in the aisles, he said it was OK this time.

— *Gerhard Dewey, MT*

As I watched a lady hustling across a muddy church yard with her arms loaded down with song books, she caught her heel in the mud and fell flat on her face. Although embarrassed, she stood up, grabbed all the books and started to run up the entry steps. She climbed the steps and as God is my witness, her slacks fell down to her ankles! (Her button & zipper must have come undone when she fell.) I laughed so hard I wet my pants!

— *Name withheld by request*

As leader of the worship band at our church, I'm in charge of providing music at our weekly services. One Sunday, near the end of one of the songs, I broke a string on my guitar. I decided not to replace it for fear of disrupting the reverent atmosphere.

I needn't have worried. When I said softly, "I hope you don't mind if I play without my G-string," the entire congregation burst out laughing.

Since our church is rather small, the pastor often holds the men's fellowship meeting in his home. When this happens, his wife retreats to their bedroom to read or watch TV.

One such get-together failed to attract many participants, so the pastor's wife got up in front of the congregation the following Sunday. Trying to drum up support for the group, she exhorted, "I want to see all of you men there. Besides, I'm not going to the bedroom for just one man!"

People in church tell me that they always feel like the whole congregation is watching them when their kids are acting up. That may be true, but really they're thinking of when their kids did the same thing (or worse) and now they can sit back and watch others.

— Don Russell, NE

Thirty years ago, when my children were very small, Sunday mornings were spent rushing around getting everyone ready. Back then, very high heels were in fashion, so I always waited to put my shoes on until we were nearly ready to leave.

One particularly hectic Sunday morning, when we finally collapsed into our church pew, imagine the horror when I looked at my feet and saw my big, fuzzy blue house slippers! I stuck my feet under the pew, wouldn't stand for the prayers, and went out the side exit when church was over.

— *Lee Ann McGregor, NE*

In the middle of the sermon, an old man belched quite loud. The preacher, engrossed in his speech hadn't heard the belch, only the laughter amongst the congregation. This laughter puzzled him, as he continued.

On his way home, the preacher popped the tape of his sermon into his cassette player, trying to find out what he had said that was so funny. He was relieved when the "belch" came across loud and clear!

— *Joyce McDuffee, NE*

Our song leader sang the words "Shall we stand and sing" to the tune of the hymn, instead of the correct words of the song.

— *Betty Andrews, OK*

While lingering in front of the Catholic church, my cousin was having one last cigarette before attending his first mass. He had never been to church, but I had finally convinced him to go with me.

As services started, I led the way inside the foyer only to turn around and see my cousin douse his cigarette in the holy water receptacle. He said he didn't know whether to throw it away outside or if there was an ash try inside. When he saw the water, he didn't know any better but thought it very convenient for the church to put one of those things there.

— *Alan Snyder, NE*

Our minister's name is Bruce Goodwin. In the bulletin's Order of Worship, he was listed as "Bruck" Goodwin as the morning speaker. It was an obvious typo, and humorist that he is, Bro. Goodwin couldn't let it go.

When he got up to the pulpit to deliver his sermon he said, "I know everyone was excited to hear my brother Bruck speak, but due to unforeseen circumstances, he can't be here today as the bulletin announced, so I will be giving the sermon as usual."

— *Ken Alley, NE*

As I walked through the church parking lot, I noticed a van that had a "JESUS" decal stuck directly above the DODGE emblem. It looked like an advertisement for "JESUS DODGE". I had never heard of this dealership, but assumed that if it was legitimate, you would be treated fairly there.

— *Ken Alley, NE*

In the middle of a sermon my friend's preacher

said, "My eyes were starting to give me trouble, so I went to my obstetrician for a check-up." His wife was pregnant for the first time, so one can understand his absent-mindedness.

— Paul Beck, NE

I had a ten-year-old cousin who would stretch out on the pew immediately after the sermon started. He would always do this and sleep until the invitation song.

One Sunday another cousin decided to tie his shoe strings together as soon as he went to sleep. As we stood to sing the invitation song, my cousin swung his feet to the floor and stood up. Right after the closing prayer he took one step out into the aisle and fell flat on his face.

Another cousin of mine tells the story of how his dad, an elder in the church, would put a song book under his elbow on the arm rest, prop his head up on his hand, lock his feet under the pew and snooze away the sermon. He did this every Sunday without fail.

One morning, after 20 minutes of listening to the sermon, my cousin decided to have some fun and knocked the book out from under his dad's elbow! This jolted his dad so much and caught him in such a slumber that he leaned forward, pitched sideways, lost his balance and fell into the center aisle.

I remember my cousin remarking that he got the worst licking of his life that afternoon.

— Rod Baxter, NE

My little three-year-old daughter was being very naughty during church, worse than usual, and to keep her still during the upcoming prayer I decided to pin her between my knees. In the quiet before the prayer she folded her hands and prayed out loud. "Dear Lord, you gotta help me, I'm trapped!"

Another time, as I stood for the benediction, I felt my daughter scrunching behind me on the pew and giving me a big hug. I thought this was sweet of her, until I felt her teeth biting my butt!

We went outside for a little chat after that episode.

— *Jan Axdahl, NE*

Before Easter I taught a pre-school class a lesson on the death, burial, and resurrection of Jesus. At one point I said, "Christ arose!"

Four-year-old Johnny went home and told his parents that I said "Christ froze!" It took two more years for him to get that right.

— *Jacae Sanders, NE*

This is one of the funniest stories I ever heard about church, although I'm quite sure it isn't true.

A timid fellow walked into the hardware store with two black eyes. The owner asked what happened and the guy said he was in church and as they stood for the benediction he noticed the lady's dress in front of him was stuck in her crack. The teenagers were laughing about this so he just leaned forward and pulled her dress out. Immediately after, the lady turned around and hit him!

This made the store owner laugh and ask, "But, how did you get the other black eye?" "Well," he explained. "As soon as I realized that I must have done something wrong, I decided to make amends and poked the dress back into her crack."

— *Arron Anderson, TX*

There was an older preacher who would reach into his pocket and get a mint to suck on while he preached. When the mint was gone, he would know his sermon was long enough and it was time to stop preaching.

One Sunday he put a button in his mouth by mistake and ended up preaching two hours before it occurred to him what he had done.

— *Alan Bailey, AR*

"The road to hell is paved with 'should haves'."

Some Fundamentalists don't have sex standing up because they're afraid it might lead to dancing.

"Sometimes one must go through hell to get to heaven."

Church doesn't change "Pain-in-the-butt people," it just gives them religion.

This lady's children were always naughty in church and one Sunday as they rose for the benediction, she grabbed one of them and whispered loudly, "Why are you kids so bad in church?"

The child thought and thought and said, "Because, Mom, we get tired of looking at big butts."

— *Lydia Romanoski, NE*

A friend of mine went into the confessional, and instead of saying the customary "Bless me, Father, for I have sinned," she absentmindedly began reciting the common table prayer, "Come, Lord Jesus, be our guest...." The priest fortunately had a terrific sense of humor, because he interrupted her and chuckled, "What'd you do, bring your lunch?"

— *Leona Martin, NE*

My little boy was very restless during Mass one Sunday. When communion started, I thought something had finally captured his interest because he calmed down and watched the front of the church intently. He was particularly charmed by the candle with the red globe hanging over the altar. Soon he was fidgeting again and plucked at my sleeve. "Mom, when is that light going to turn green so we can go?" he whispered.

— *Leona Martin, NE*

On the way home from a funeral, my 5-year-old son asked, "Dad, did the priest really say 'In the name of the Father, Son and in the hole she goes'?"

— *Bob Simon, NM*

I remember when the preacher's kids took their dad's sermon notes out of his Bible Sunday morning and replaced them with comic book pages. As I recall, the church floors were sure polished for a long time after that incident.

— *Keith Heppner, NE*

A friend of mine was taking her young son to confession. When she told him, for some reason he seemed overjoyed and very excited. When they got to church and walked inside she found out the reason. He thought she had said they were goin' fishin'.

— *Linda Loge, NE*

A preacher's kid said at a church social, "Dad preaches in his underwear." Of course he denied it, "I do not!" "Do too!" "Do not!" on and on they carried on, until the kid said, "Don't you put on your underwear before your suit pants?" (Kids!)

— *Keith Heppner, NE*

My 4-year-old son was watching the priest walk down the aisle and he said, "Mom, look, there's Hallelujah!"

— *Pat Brinkman, NE*

I was in church one day and towards the end of the service my daughter whispered to me, "Dad, your shirt's inside out."

— *Al Kenly, WA*

My priest pushes up his glasses with his middle finger. It looks a little funny when he does this during his sermon.

— *Bob Abrams, CT*

At a large fish fry, a brother in Christ asked "How long have you been preaching?" When I told him, my younger brother, whom I had been trying to convert for some time, said "Huh! He's been preaching a lot longer than that, he's just getting paid for it now."

— *Marvin Greene, KS*

HEY, SEND ME YOUR STORIES!

Chapter 5

Wedding and Marriage Oops

While doing a wedding rehearsal for my brother and his fiance, I came to the part of asking the father "Who gives this daughter away?" I was looking at the fiance's mother and said "Who gives this mother away?" It woke everyone up, including myself.

— *Mike Potts, TX*

While kneeling in front of the pastor, the shoe soles of the groom said,

H	E
L	P

I now "announce" you man and wife.

"Will you take this man to be your wife?"

At this wedding, the seven-year-old ring bearer and the four-year-old flower girl were brother and sister. Before the ceremony started their dad told his son to make sure his sister got down the aisle with the flowers. Big brother ended up dragging her, because she wasn't coming!

— *Gary Groteluschen, NE*

One of the bridesmaids got her heel stuck in the heat grate and continued without either shoe on.

— Gary Groteluschen, NE

I was at a marriage ceremony when the groom fainted and had to be held up by the best man.

— Vaughn Domeier, NE

During this ceremony, the groom was so emotional that he couldn't recite his vows. The pastor had to change things so he would have to just nod his head, yes or no.

— Lydia Romanowski, NE

This ceremony was being taped when my husband, the pastor, put the microphone in front of the groom to recite his vows. The groom was so nervous he leaned forward and said "Hello."

— Lydia Romanowski, NE

The bride fainted during this ceremony and the groom had to carry her out. At least she waited till the end.

— James Tyler, IN

Before each of my friend's children got married, she would make them eat their favorite meal 10 times in a row, just to show them how true feelings can change, and how careful they should be when choosing a mate.

— Jane Tohnson, IA

The sign on the back of the newlywed's car read, "Just Marred."

"Those whom God has joined together, let no one put us under."
— *Bobby James, SC*

Bumper sticker: Don't criticize your wife. If she were perfect, she would have married better.
— *Warren Dier, OK*

While at a large wedding in a huge church, I decided to take the elevator ride to the balcony. While I was waiting, and goof-off that I can be, as the elevator door opened I said "BOO!" to the person who was directly inside. It happened to be one of the bridesmaids and I startled her so much that she screamed and broke wind at the same time. She was so embarrassed she just walked away without saying a word. I didn't mean to scare her like that, honest!
— *William O'Dell, IL*

My roommate was to be married to a young man from the city we were living in. While growing up, she had lived in many states and several countries and had not had a chance to experience the camaraderie and high jinks of close family and lifetime friends. The groom's friends planned to remedy that and give her a post-wedding treat she would remember. The wedding and the getaway from the church went as planned. The happy couple sped around town with the best man driving and several cars in chase with horns blaring. Suddenly the best man drove downtown and pulled into a large parking lot one-half block off main street. The best man had been bought off and he had duly delivered the bride to family and friends (who had cut across town) for the second major event of the evening. Armed with a parade permit and a wheelbarrow, the entire party proceeded to main street with the bride in her gown and the groom in formal attire. Once there, the bride was required (compelled) to wheel the groom down the middle of the street for two blocks with traffic stopped everywhere. Imagine the noise and attention that generated. A carefully placed phone call guaranteed that the local TV station would be there. The entire event was wrapped up in time for the ten o'clock news.

— *Judi Domeier, NE*

At our wedding in my wife's church, I found out a little too late that the minister was fond of last-minute pranks. The male members of the wedding party and the minister entered from the pastor's study. I was last before the minister and he gave me just enough of a shove that I stumbled coming through the door. At the reception, family members said I appeared to have taken some liquid courage or the minister was pushing in a reluctant groom.

— *Vaughn Domeier, NE*

"I now pronounce you male and female."

My six-year-old son said he was going to be the ring "barrier" at my wedding next month.

— *Sherri Oberg, NE*

After the wedding, we went down to the basement of the church for the reception. There was a big bowl of red punch on the table, and my son said, "Look Mom, they like Bloody Marys just like you do!"

— *Chris Tonniges, NE*

The bride was wearing an old lace gown which fell to the floor as she came down the aisle.

Right after the "I do's" in our wedding ceremony, the old priest unfolded a beautiful white napkin, (I assumed for use in our communion service). He proceeded to honk his nose in it so loud that all in attendance cracked up laughing.

— *Angel Fiegener, NE*

The young pastor, now a Lutheran chaplain in South Dakota, was beaming, as were the bride and groom before him. All had gone well with this, his first wedding. In waiting for the recessional to begin, he leaned over to ask the bride if she wanted to kiss. With that, she leaned over the altar rail, gave the pastor a kiss, then took the groom by the arm and marched out — leaving a very red-faced pastor behind.

— *David Webster, MN*

At a recent wedding the groom was 15 minutes late. Turning on my portable mike, I headed out to announce to the congregation that the groom had been contacted and that the wedding would take place in another 15 minutes. In the hall I met the custodian and photographer and said couples should pay more attention to wedding times than flowers. This was fine except my mike was on and the congregation overheard the custodian complaining about the lateness of the wedding and his other obligations and so I announced to the congregation, "We should get time and a half for this wedding!" The congregation approved laughingly! Then I proceeded to announce, "I have enough time, I'm going to the bathroom." At the sound of rushing water, one of the parishioners ran down the aisle and yelled into the bathroom and partially over the mike. "Your mike is on!" The most painful part of this experience was having to face all those people with their huge grins when the groom did arrive and the wedding began.

— *James Leipold, CT*

HEY, SEND ME YOUR STORIES!

Chapter 6

Things Pondered During Dry Sermons

Some people sow their oats on Saturday night, and pray for crop failure Sunday morning.

Is Murphy's Law the same as "what you sow, so shall you reap?"

If loud children bother you in church, odds are you are sitting in the back.

Instead of buying the boy a Bible, they told him his name was Gideon, and took one from a motel.

Why does the preacher always get long-winded on the Sunday you need to be somewhere else by noon?

Idleness is the devil's playhouse.

What exactly can a mortuary screw up?

It seems that some families are breeding their own Youth Group.

Some children wonder how God keeps from falling out of heaven, and if the angels are really bowling when it thunders and crying when it rains.

If there's nothing good to say about Satan, how come the phrase "You Lucky Devil" is so popular?

People who trust in God to take care of their backs forget that God's main interest is their souls, not their posture.

Worship is not a spectator sport, it is a participation sport.

If you have to be baptized in order to baptize someone else, who baptized the first Christian?

Funny how big a $20 bill looks in the collection plate but how small it looks at the supermarket.

How many people who don't go to church have the same name? I'm "too tired."

Funny how long an hour seems in worship but how short it seems when golfing, fishing, or watching a ball game.

Sign in restaurant: In God We Trust, All Others Pay Cash!

Funny how laborious it is to read a chapter in the Bible but how easy it is to read a 300 page novel.

I wonder if anyone has ever poured bubble bath in the baptistry?

I know I belong to the right church, because my family can get to the Sunday buffets before other churches are out.

God created man. Col. Colt made them equal, as the saying goes.

Funny how people scramble to get a front seat at the ball park, but grab a back seat at church.

After you change something with your golf grip that makes for a perfect shot, don't you feel a little silly thinking you did it all by yourself?

Thinking about all the different preachers I've heard brings back such nodstalgia.

Being rich isn't a sin, it's a miracle.

If the patient lives, the doctor gets all the credit. If the patient dies, it's God's will. Hey, sounds like a great job!

Some people think heaven is a place you can't get to from here.

What are you listening for when you hear the hush of the congregation?

If you don't feel as close to God as you once did, who moved?

Our church didn't have any additions last year, but we had some blessed subtractions.

Yes, God has a sense of humor: listen to how he made some people sing.

Happiness is waking up with the drudgery of going to work, and then remembering it's Sunday.

When you can't locate that wasp in church, do you ever feel like it's landed on your head?

I'm so tired of those sermons on patience!

Isn't it fun watching other parents' kids in church?

While in church, don't the parents of crying children hear them?

Does the preacher really have to speak so long to get his message across?

Why do people who pray for patience want it right now?

If Jesus would have been stoned to death, would Catholics have to hit themselves instead of making the sign of the Cross?

Bumper sticker: Why didn't Noah just swat those two mosquitoes?

Are buffets a sin? (They are to me).

God creates; man rearranges.

Bumper sticker: TRUST IN GOD —
                 SHE WILL PROVIDE

Bumper sticker: DON'T BE CAUGHT DEAD
                 WITHOUT JESUS!

Is Purgatory the 100 feet between the "Leaving Nebraska" sign and the "Entering Kansas" sign?

"We'll never forget this book for a long time."

If Sunday does not open a door to higher things it is apt to be a trap to lower.

It is better to be religious with your eloquence than it is to be eloquent with your religion.

Folks do not get to heaven on goodness who were good for lack of opportunity to be bad.

The farmer has learned that he cannot sow and reap the same day. Some city folks don't know it yet.

We certainly would like to have heard the excuse Eve gave her neighbors for moving out of Eden.

A restless tongue is twin sister to the devil's tail.

Heavenly stars never speak of their dazzling brilliance.

Church membership is not an elevator into heaven.

You can tell about how a child will turn out if you know what time they turn in.

No man is going to walk straight who is watching his neighbor.

Too many people to whom God has given wings are complaining of corns.

Some men put a couple of dollars in the collection plate for the same reason that they buy a lightning rod.

The rocks we hold to throw at our neighbor have a way of getting into our own pillows.

Folks who do their religious duties by proxy must be willing to take their rewards in the same way.

The hypocrites are always hard on the heretics.

Preacher, do you have something to say, or do you just have to say something?

When the conscience of a man speaks it says, "You've been found out."

Some folks try to measure the goodness of God by the yardstick of their own charity.

You can hide your light under a bushel all you please, but you've got to pay the gas bill just the same.

A lot of the pearls that people cast before swine are imitation.

It is usually the rich that say to the poor, "Be of good cheer."

When you get the daily bread you have been praying for, do not grumble because it is not cake.

The world will not be convinced of your faith by the sourness of your face.

Some say, "Get thee behind me Satan" and put him in their hip pocket.

Patience is considered a virtue when it often is merely a case of not knowing what to do.

The most striking sermon is usually the one that hits the man who is not there.

A man does not stumble over the moral law until he tries to cross it.

The men who serve the world are never worried as to whether you are watching their smoke.

It is hard to choose between a dainty saint and a dirty sinner.

Some men cast their bread upon the waters with a string tied to it.

When a man has an excuse for a wrong, he usually has a use for it.

When you hear a puffing preacher, get out of his track.

Half of wisdom is being silent when you have nothing to say.

It is but a short step from the critical to the hypocritical.

Some men think they are saints because they are selective in their sins.

Things too small to pray over may be great enough to sin over.

The water of life is not enriched by running through the mud of our bigotry.

You cannot slay one devil by raising another.

It makes all the difference whether the shepherd loves the fleece or the flock.

Where the devil is free to take the hindermost, he will not fear to take the foremost.

Many put zero into the collection and then complain that the church is cold.

God said let there be light — and pushed the button.

The best place to criticize your neighbor is in front of your own mirror.

There is more hope of a self-convicted sinner than there is of a self-conceited saint.

Too many expect to purchase heaven with the profits made by selling their own soul.

The child is not likely to find a father in God unless he finds something of God in his father.

It may be easier to write a guide book to heaven than it is to go there.

It makes a poor dish to mix the garlic of Egypt with the honey of Canaan.

There is no promise of a robe of righteousness to the man who gives away his old overcoat in July.

The worst of all liars may be able to make the best analysis of truth.

There will be some people in the front seats in heaven that you would not admit to your pew here.

Fishers of men need to prepare their bait for another fish besides suckers.

Some men who are boasting of their sand do not realize that it is all in their foundations.

Don't salt and pepper religion; take your soul food straight.

When you loan four dollars to a human saint your faith is worth four dollars.

You need the church and the church needs you; to fill your place it will take two.

The church needs less block and more tackle.

Religion that controls one's heart and hand can easily convince another's head.

The Christian on his knees sees more than the philosopher on tiptoe.

God often has a great share in a little house, and a little share in a great house.

You can't take your money to heaven with you, but you can send it on ahead of you.

The only sermon the devil really fears is the living one on two legs.

Showers of blessings are not called down by thunders of oratory.

The atheist cannot find God for the same reason that a thief cannot find a policeman.

Don't judge a man by the clothes he wears; God made one, the tailor the other.

Don't judge a man by his family relation; Cain belonged to a good family.

A willing church worker is never without a job.

If God is your partner, make your plans large.

Chapter 7

Contributions

The following excerpts are taken, with the permission from the author, from the book titled, LIFE, HUMOR, and BIBLICAL BRIEFS, by J.A. McNutt. I highly recommend this book and it can be purchased by contacting: MACS PUBLICATIONS, 3040 East Road, Memphis, Tenn. 38128 — $13.50.

When I first came to Coleman Avenue church in Memphis, the elders proposed to give me half of the Sunday's contribution as my salary. This was in the midst of the depression and support proved to be pretty small, but as the congregation grew the contribution increased and it was decided by some that the preacher was getting too much money. At my own request, they cut my income by putting me on a regular salary. Later brother W.J. Winn loved to tell that I was the only preacher that he had ever known who preached on commission.

While I was preaching in Arkansas, one Sunday after the morning worship service, the telephone rang, and the lady charged me with making a certain statement in my sermon. I tried to tell her that she evidently misunderstood, and that I had not made the statement. When she insisted that I had done so, my reply was, "Lady, I never believed that in my life, and I am not accustomed to saying things that I don't believe."

In warning men not to think more highly of themselves than they ought to think, I have enjoyed telling the story of the young preacher who had waxed eloquent in his sermon, and had shown an evident lack of humility in reciting his accomplishments. His ego was really deflated by one of the elderly sisters, who asked, "Son, has anyone ever told you how wonderful you are?" When he replied, "No sister Jones," she punctured his ego by saying, "How did you find it out?"

It was brother H. Leo Boles, a great gospel preacher, and one time editor of the Gospel Advocate and president of David Lipscomb College, who said, "I wish that all my preaching brethren could preach the gospel better than I can." Now contrast this with the attitude of another preacher who said, "I won't let any preacher preach the gospel better than I can."

Carl Ketcherside was criticizing me continually in his speeches, when finally during a break in the proceedings, I had an opportunity to respond. I told the audience, "Please don't think hard of Carl because of the things he has been saying about me. It reminds me of the case of the little hundred pound woman who was charged with beating her husband, and the judge couldn't understand it because the husband weighed at least two hundred pounds. So he asked the husband, "Why would a big fellow like you let a little woman like this beat up on you?" His reply was, "Well, judge, you see it don't hurt me none, and she gets a lot of pleasure out of it." The audience had a big laugh, and Ketcherside ceased to be so critical.

The head begins to swell when the mind quits growing.

Alcohol kills the living and preserves the dead.

In the early days while holding a meeting in Eagle Lake, Florida, I was interrupted by a hobby riding brother who arose in the audience and insisted on having something to say. It was apparent that he intended to try to embarrass me and take over the service. I proceeded to ask, "What congregation do you attend and what church will endorse you?" When he could not name such a congregation, I simply asked that he be seated, since he only represented himself, and I would talk to him at the conclusion of my sermon.

A man on my brother-in-law's farm was a religious man, and a zealous member of the Baptist church. He mentioned that his friend Frank was now a deacon in the Baptist church. When my brother-in-law replied, "I didn't know Frank was a deacon," he replied, "Yes sir, he's done been crowned." I don't know what kind of ceremony was involved, but I have seen a few deacons that needed to be crowned.

One of my favorite stories concerning brother J.D. Tant is about the time he was preaching in a gospel meeting at Coleman Avenue in Memphis, Tennessee,

in the early days. It is said that one of our more intel-
lectual and sophisticated preachers was asked to lead
the prayer this night, and he used so many words
beyond the comprehension of the average audience
that brother Tant responded by saying, "John, I hope
that the Lord understood what you were saying
because I didn't get a word of it."

The little boy was walking slowly along the sidewalk
when one of the town's skeptics asked, "Where have
you been this morning?" When the little fellow
replied, "I have been to Sunday School to learn about
God," the man said, "I have a brand new dime that I
will give you if you will tell me where God is." The boy
thought about the question a moment and then came
his reply. "Mister, I will give you a dollar if you can tell
me where God ain't."

A good thing about telling the truth is that you
don't have to remember what you said.

Someone has said large churches are churches
where no one knows anyone else and they are glad
they don't, and small churches are churches where
everybody knows everybody else and they are sorry
they do.

While preaching for the church in Paragould,
Arkansas, I had a daily radio show in which we try to
present the gospel in a positive way, but whenever necessary to expose religious error, we did not hesitate to

defend the truth. This of course resulted in some religious controversy, so the station owner suggested one day, "Brother Mac, if you would just preach the truth instead of condemning other teachings, you would have a more popular program." To which I replied, "Yes, I am fully aware of that, and if I owned the radio station as you do, I would want the widest popular approval possible, but I have a higher duty than gaining popularity for the program or myself, and that is to please the Lord by condemning sin and exposing false doctrine." He looked me in the eye and smiled as he said, "I knew you were going to say that."

A church member once bragged, "If I had a million dollars I'd gladly give the church half of it."
An elder said, "If you had two dollars, would you give one of them to the church."
The member replied, "That's not fair, you knew I had two dollars."

Two surgeons were performing an operation on a patient when a house just outside the hospital operating room caught fire. As the flames mounted up higher, one doctor said to the other, "John, you had better lower the window shade, our patient may wake up and think that this operation wasn't a success."

My good friend and brother, Cleo E. Wallace, was an avid golfer and he told me that on one occasion he was playing golf with a Methodist preacher who hit a ball into the lake. Seeing his ball disappear beneath the water the preacher said, "Well, I really baptized that one." Brother Wallace replied, "Strange that you can't understand that when you baptize someone."

I would like to hear a sermon on the ten commandments by one of our brethren who never, never does any negative preaching.

Soft soap in the pulpit won't cleanse the sinner in the pew.

Drunkenness is nothing more than voluntary madness. (Seneca)

O God, that men should put an enemy in their mouths to steal away their brains. (Shakespeare)

Many people are under the impression that the only difference between churches of Christ and Christian Churches is the use or non-use of instrumental music. While in college I had an appointment to preach in a small town, where I had never been before. When I got off the bus near the courthouse, I started out to look for the church building, and meeting one of the local citizens I asked, "Where is the church of Christ?" His reply was in the form of another question, "Fiddlers, or non-fiddlers?"

Too many of us are like the Scotsman who said, "God grant that I may always be right, because I never change."

Perhaps you have heard the story of the man at church who, during the sermon, went to sleep and fell off the pew and broke his arm. He went to his lawyer and wanted to sue the church, but the lawyer advised against suing the church saying, "You can't win a suit against the church, but you can sue the preacher for administering an anesthetic without a license."

Perhaps you have heard the story about the old preacher who was involved in a meeting where rainy weather was about to cancel the attendance and he reportedly said, "It is the Lord's meeting, and the Lord's weather, so if he wants to rain out his own meeting, there's nothing I can do about it."

"Every tub should set on its own bottom." That's not in the Bible, but it ought to be.

In one of my early efforts at holding a protracted meeting in a rural area of Mississippi, the services were being interrupted by loud talking outside the building one night. Instead of dealing with the situation in such a way as to provoke more interference, I simply spoke up loud enough to be heard outside and said, "Listen fellows, we have some brethren who are accustomed to taking a nap during services, and if you don't quit talking so loud you are going to wake them up." Laughter was heard outside and there was no further problem during the meeting.

It is easy to ruin a good bird dog by lending him to strangers. It seems that a fellow had a real first class dog named "Deacon" that was a real good worker in the field trials. He really covered the ground and pointed more birds than some of the best dogs in the country, but some fellows borrowed him for a hunt. They got confused on his name and started calling him "Preacher" and he hasn't done one thing since.

A young man saw a beautiful young lady and was so attracted to her that it was love at first sight. He wanted her for his wife, so he went to his room and began praying to God to help him win her as his bride. However, his prayers were not effective and it seems that God said no to his request.

Fifteen years passed by and then one day he was walking down the street and met the same girl. She was now fifteen years older, and he returned to his room and thanked the Lord for having said "No" to his prayer.

I am told that brother JD Tant was preparing to baptize a fellow in a pond or creek, when the man reached in his hip pocket to retrieve his pocket book and hand it to a friend on the bank. Brother Tant responded by saying, "Put that back in your pocket, I want to baptize it too!" In the course of more than fifty years as a gospel preacher I have observed that we have quite a few "unbaptized pocketbooks" among our brethren.

I heard the story from one of my brethren of an incident that occurred there while brother JD Tant was preaching in a meeting. It seems that while brother Tant was speaking, an old hound dog planted his feet on the front steps of the building and began to howl, whereupon brother Tant ceased to preach and made this request, "Brethren, one of you go out there and kill that dog. He may be called to preach, but this is my appointment."

While preaching at the Second and Walnut Sts. church building one Sunday morning, in my enthusiasm I had exceeded the usual time limits for the sermon, much to the dislike of one of my elderly brethren. Perhaps he had heard the sermon before, and besides he was getting hungry, which provoked his comment. Anyway, the old brother extracted his pocket watch, looked at it closely, put it back in his pocket, and observed to a friend nearby, "Time for dinner ain't it?" I heard the comment up in the pulpit and decided it was time to conclude.... How could I have done otherwise?

Perhaps you have heard of the preacher who was troubled by the negative attitude, continued criticism, harassment, and objections of one of the deacons, who closed the worship services with these words, "We will now be led in a few words of criticism by brother Jones."

Some church members who love to sing, "I'm standing on the Promises," are merely sitting on the premises.

It has been said that the cooing usually stops when the honeymoon is over, but the billing goes on forever.

Perhaps you have heard of the engaged couple who broke up for religious reasons. It seems that she was a worshipper of money, and he didn't have any.

The new preacher had arrived to work with the church, and the officials were holding a ceremony in which they kept referring to installing the preacher. The little boy sitting next to his father didn't quite understand what was happening so he turned to his father and said, "Do they mean to put him in a stall and feed him?" In reply, the father said, "No, son, they just hitch him to the church and expect him to pull it."

Many a man in love with a dimple has made the mistake of marrying the whole girl.

If you don't want the fruits of sin, stay out of the orchard.

A religious awakening is what takes place after the preacher finishes his sermon.

Some men are born meek, and others get married.

An old brother was having so many problems, and faced trouble he was unable to deal with, so he decided to talk to the Lord about the matter. He left the house and went down to the pasture, knelt down under an old oak tree and began telling the Lord about his troubles. While he was praying, a bird splattered his bald head, and the old fellow arose and said, "See there Lord, that's what I have been telling you. They sing for some people."

Some people's minds are like concrete.... All mixed up and permanently set.

Brother John Gibson of Little Rock, Arkansas, ran this little story in his church bulletin. It seems that some boys were continually crossing a field, and the farmer decided to stop them by erecting a "No Trespassing" sign on his land. This made one of the boys so angry that he vowed that he would get even with the farmer, so he went to the feed store, bought a supply of Johnson grass seed, and sowed every field, fully. Later on he fell in love with the farmer's daughter, and they were married. When the old man died, he inherited the farm and spent the rest of his life fighting Johnson grass. And if you don't understand the situation, you've never lived on a farm.

What the world, and many of the brethren, wants is a bowl of ice cream with a cherry on it, but what the world and the brethren need is a bowl of beans with an onion on it.

Shortly after moving to Oklahoma to work with the Central church in that city, I was officiating a church wedding. My wife came into the auditorium and took a seat in the middle of the building to witness the ceremony. Soon after she was seated, a young lady moved in and sat down beside her and whispered, "How do you like the new preacher?" Whereupon my wife answered softly, "I must like him pretty well, I have been married to him for seventeen years."

Many a mother has spent 21 years making a man out of her son, only to see some other woman make a monkey out of him in an hour or so.

The evangelist had just returned for his second meeting with the same church, when he was approached by a man who was evidently inebriated. He greeted the preacher with considerable enthusiasm saying, "Don't you know me brother Brown? I am one of your converts of last summer." To which the preacher replied, "You must be, because I'm certain that the Lord didn't have anything to do with it."

THE FOLLOWING ARE BORROWED WITH PERMISSION FROM "THE LUTHERAN WITNESS" MAGAZINE and OTHERS:

Asked by his father how he liked his first day at vacation Bible school, the four-year-old said, "Just great. We go outside to play, and when we come back in, God has juice and cookies all ready."
— *Shepherd of the Hills Church, Ont.*

While telling the story of the first Christmas, our

168

church's nursery-school teacher asked her class, "What did the angel say to Mary?

No one answered at first, but then little Stephen piped up: "That God was going to be a Daddy soon!"
— *Redeemer Lutheran Church, NJ*

A pastor asked the youngsters in his children's religion class to define certain churchly terms. Here are the results:

Absolution: Making sure you're right.

Conversion: The point after a touchdown.

Epistle: The wife of an apostle.

False doctrine: Giving someone the wrong medicine.

Hymn: The bottom of a lady's dress.

Redemption: Getting something with green stamps.
— *The Lutheran Church of Our Savior, OK*

A church that prided itself on good fellowship always served coffee after services. One morning, the pastor asked my little daughter if she knew why they served the coffee. "Yes," she said, "It's to help people to get wide awake before driving home."
— *Bethel Lutheran Church, CA*

"The sermon's all done?" asked the latecomer of the pastor at the church door.

"The sermon has been preached," said the pastor. "It remains to be done."
— *The Lutheran Church of Our Savior, OK*

A little boy was gazing into the crib at his new baby sister, who was lying there crying loudly.

"Did she come from heaven?" the boy asked his mother.

"Yes," the mother said tenderly, "she did."

"Well, with all that noise she's making," he retorted, "It's no wonder they threw her out."

— *Our Savior Lutheran Church, TX*

"Redemption Center: No Stamps Required" was the message on the signboard outside Huntington Woods Lutheran Church.

The Sunday school lesson for the nursery-age class concerned the fact that Jesus is always with us, even when we can't see him. "I know that already," piped one of the four-year-olds. "He's the one who opens the doors at the grocery store."

— *George V. Kottwitz, IL*

Frustrated because of poor attendance at rehearsals, the choir director called for attention at the last rehearsal before Easter, saying, "I wish to publicly thank the tenor for being the only member of the choir to attend every rehearsal."

"It was the least I could do," the tenor replied, "since I won't be here for Easter."

— *Lutheran Church of Our Savior, OK*

Our son-in-law is a pastor in the Oklahoma panhandle. Some weeks ago he received a call to another congregation. We were anxious to know whether he would accept it. Finally, his six-year-old called with the news: "Daddy,' he announced, "has reclined it."

— *George Kottwitz, IL*

We sing "Sweet Hour of Prayer" and are content with five minutes a day.

We sing "Onward Christian Soldiers" and wait to be drafted into his service.

We sing "O For A Thousand Tongues to Sing" and don't use the one we have.

We sing "Blest Be The Tie That Binds" and let the least little offense sever it.

We sing "Serve The Lord With Gladness" and gripe about all we have to do.

We sing "We're Marching to Zion" but fail to march to worship or Sunday School.

We sing "I Love To Tell The Story" and never mention it at all.

— *The Lutheran Church of Our Savior, OH*

More children's responses on "What Is A Pastor?"

"He's a Jesus man. He prays for us and shows ya movies."

"He's a good man with nice, nice, nice, neat shoes."

"He's somebody we sit by who wears white blouses and he washes his hands at the altar."

"He's a church man. He has a black suit and a tie thing and he combs his hair."

"He's the one upstairs who cleans up lots of messes."

"He reads books and tells stories and tells people what to do and he shakes your hand, too."

"He wears a black thing that goes all the way down to your toes."

"He's God, and he wears God clothes and prays a lot and talks a lot."

"I don't know what pastors are, but I do know about airplanes. They fly."

— *Christ Lutheran Church, MO*

The kindergarten teacher at our school was reviewing the events of Palm Sunday with her students. She mentioned how even the children waving palm branches sang "Hosanna!"

With this, little Jason spoke up: "I know that one! 'O, Hosanna, oh don't you cry for me!...'"

A father was teaching his young son what a Christian should be like. When the lesson was finished, the father got a spiritual stab that he never forgot: "Daddy," asked the boy, "have I ever seen a Christian?"

— *Shepherd of the Hills Church, WI*

My husband, a pastor, keeps a box in his car with tracts, a private communion set and a small Bible for making visits. On a recent trip, our seven-year-old daughter was paging through the Bible and asked, "Does Problems come before or after Romans?"

— *Kim Bell, MI*

After telling the story of Samuel's anointing of young David to be king of Israel, I asked a class of third graders if anyone knew why the old prophet poured oil on David's head.

"Sure," replied one lad. "To make the crown slip on easier!"

The four-year-old boy watched carefully as members of the congregation dropped their offerings into the plate. When the plate approached his father, he whispered, "Don't pay for me, Daddy. Remember, I'm still under five."
— *Faith Lutheran Church, Ont.*

Rev. Tom Fast was recently installed as pastor of First Lutheran Church, Natchez, Miss. His new circuit counselor is Rev. Rod Loose. Thus, the district now features a couple of pastors who are Fast and Loose.

Our preacher, addressing the congregation, began his sermon thus: "My job this morning, as I understand it, is to talk to you; yours, as I understand it, is to listen. If you finish before I do, just hold up your hand."
— *Trinity Lutheran Church, TX*

The offering was in progress. The two ushers reached each end of the pew in front of us simultaneously, but failed to synchronize their duties. Both started their respective basket down the same pew.

That suggested a collision, but when the baskets reached the center, a graceful young matron, never missing a beat, took one in each hand, crossing one over the other, and continued them on their way.

She did have a trace of a grin on her face, and I'm sure a twinkle in her eyes. So did we in the pew behind her.

— North Wisconsin Lutheran Newsletter

When I was a young pastor, an older preacher told me that if I ever forgot the marriage ceremony, I should start quoting scripture until I remembered.

Sure enough, when performing my second wedding, I forgot the words. However, the only scripture I could remember was, "Father, forgive them, for they know not what they do."

Not long ago, our family attended a wedding. The next day our four-year-old daughter was playing wedding with her dolls. From the next room, I overheard her say, "Do you take this woman to be your awfully lovely wife?"

An announcement about a congregational cookbook recently ran in our worship bulletin. "Please submit your favorite recipe," the notice read, "along with a short antidote concerning it."

— George Kottwitz, IL

Our pastor's sermon, "Are Selfishness and Greed Replacing Thankfulness and Gratitude?" was truly inspiring. He wrapped it up by boldly challenging the members of the congregation to give mightily of their financial gifts. Unfortunately, the offering was delayed

when the ushers couldn't find the collection plates.
— *St. John's Lutheran Church, MN*

Little Andy was miffed when he didn't get the part he wanted in the Sunday School Christmas pageant. He had hoped for the role of Joseph but got stuck with being the innkeeper instead.

During dress rehearsal, he decided to pull a fast one to get even. So, when Mary and Joseph came to his place seeking shelter, he said, "Sure folks, come right in. Plenty of room."

The perplexed children playing Mary and Joseph entered and were shown around. But then Joseph, equal to the occasion, said, "Hey, this place is a dump! We'd rather sleep in the stable!"
— *George Kottwitz, IL*

As my wife was giving our newborn his bath, my daughter came running to me and hollered, "Dad, BJ's biblical cord fell off!"
— *David Munn, NE*

THE FOLLOWING ARE BORROWED WITH PER-MISSION FROM THE "LUTHERAN" MAGAZINE AND OTHERS:

During the children's sermon, the pastor asked, "Who knows what is going to be happening on Good Friday?" A young boy raised his hand and said, "I know. That's when spring break starts!"
— *Marjorie Munson, OH*

This license plate was spotted in Bellevue, Washington: I DODQYR. It belongs to a choir director and stands for: "I do dee choir."

Los Angeles Times readers were startled to see the following headline: ST. JOHN PLEADS NO CONTEST TO DRUNK DRIVING until they learned it was a lady's last name and she was given a fine of $1,175 and four years probation.

CHURCH PARKING ONLY—Limited to official church business. Violators' vehicles spirited away at owner's expense.

I overheard a little girl pray, "Lead a snot into temptation, but deliver us from evil."

Seeking to reactivate the church men's group, a few members were trying to think of possible names for the group. Someone said, "How about Men of St. Timothy? Then we could be known as MOST." Someone else responded, "I doubt the ladies will borrow this idea for their group. Then they would be known as LOST."

— *Clair Hoifjeld, PA*

"NEEDED: Love seat for counseling center."

ENJOY GROUP SINGING?
"INCHOIR" WITHIN!!

Since I work as a university costumer, I was able to help a local congregation to prepare for their re-enactment of the Lord's Supper. On the day after the performance I returned to my shop to find the costumes and a note: "Thanks for all your help." It was signed, "Jesus Christ and the 12 apostles."

Sign in a nursery
"We shall not all sleep, but we shall all be changed."
— I Corinthians 15:51

I couldn't help but be amused by the sign on the Presbyterian Church: "WATER SHORTAGE? WE SPRINKLE!"

Recently some yard-less friends asked if they could bury their cat in our yard. After they had gone, I insisted my eight-year-old daughter join me in placing a cross on the grave. "Daddy, is that cat a Lutheran?" she asked. "I don't know," I answered. After a few minutes of pondering she responded, "I know, Daddy, it probably was a Catlick!"

Supply houses serving this church are startled when they see that their honorarium checks are signed by the church treasurer "Robin Hood."
— *Charles Naugle, PA*

One kid thought the Golden Rule was, "Never let them see you sweat."

A wall plaque in church says, "Never give up." Right next to it at the same eye level is a box in large letters, "OLD HYMNALS."

At this church, after repair of the drinking fountain, which had long suffered with poor water pressure, the following sign was placed above it:

IF THOU PRESSETH TOO HARD UPON
THE BUTTON, THOU SHALT BE
REMINDED OF THY BAPTISM

During Lent, I asked my Sunday School class what they understood about "penance." After silence, one boy's face lit up as he answered, "That's what I got hanging on my bedroom wall!"
— *William Oyler, MN*

My 6-year-old daughter has her own idea of biblical inerrancy. One day, out of the blue, she asked, "Why doesn't the Bible say, 'By God' on the cover?"
— *Sharon L. Norlander, MN*

While putting items in my files at Southern Ohio Correctional Facility where I am chaplain, I became aware of two folders in sequence in my drawer. The first is "Death Notices" followed by "Gate Authorizations."
— *O. Franklin Johnson, OH*

I was excited about my son's coming ordination. I asked the Rev. if he could recommend a good book for

the father of a future minister. He disappeared for a few seconds. When he returned he handed me a Bible!
— *Larry Ludford, MS*

A mother told this story at our adult Sunday School class. She and some friends were discussing the differences between their denomination's beliefs and practices. One woman said, "If you're a Baptist, you always carry your Bible to church." Another said, "The Catholics have to take their rosaries." Then the mother's 8-year-old daughter chimed in, "It's easy being a Lutheran. All we have to bring is our checkbook."
— *Lisa Ubbelohde, PA*

A Baltimore store recently displayed a beautiful Italian-crafted Nativity scene. In the manger where baby Jesus was to be was a small sign that said, "Baby Jesus available upon request." Is there something theological in that?
— *David Schafer, VA*

Upon being introduced to the pastor and told he is "the minister in charge of this church," one of the preschoolers at St. Luke Lutheran Church, Farmingdale, NY, piped up, "NO-o-o...GOD's in charge."
— *Terri Shizume, NY*

During vacation church school, one of the classes was playing the Bible Times Trivia Game. the question came up, "What game did they play in Egypt?" the correct answer was marbles, but a sharp student replied, "The $25,000 Pyramid."

— *Ken Voglerr, IN*

At First Lutheran Church, Clear Lake, Wisconsin, youth under 10 may accompany their parents to the communion table to receive a blessing from the pastor. Grandma Anita recently asked her grandson, "Would you like to go up to the altar with me?" After thinking about it for a moment, he responded, "No. But will you bring me back a cracker?"

— *Roy N. Gustafson, WI*

To keep my younger son quiet in church, I always supply him with a pencil and paper. But I wasn't sure he always paid attention to what was going on during the service. One Sunday the service was especially long with extra hymns and a baptism. After lunch the boys went out into the backyard to play. After a while I heard the sound of water coming from the bathroom. Going to investigate, I saw my son standing by the sink clutching a large grasshopper in one hand and a small bar of soap in the other. He held it under the water and said, "I baptize you in the name of the Father, Son, and the Holy Soap." He HAD been listening in church!

— *Lynn Hicks, OK*

One of our 4-year-old members greeted me following our worship service during this year's Olympics. She said, "Hi, pastor. I see the cross that is hanging around your neck is silver. You must be in second place."

— Paul M. Youngdale, MN

The question for the confirmand was: "Jesus spoke with a _____ at a well about living water." The hoped-for response was "Samaritan woman." The unexpected response from one confirmand was "Southern accent."

— Keith Muschinse, WI

Three-year-old Gregory Robinson was costumed as a miniature shepherd for Bethlehem Lutheran Church, Longmont, Colorado's outdoor living Nativity scene. When his mother asked if he'd like to participate next Christmas, Gregory said, "Yes. But next year I'd rather be a pirate."

— Jonathan & Jouanne Isernhagen, CO

To give a personal touch to the gift my daughter brought to her Sunday School teacher, I decided to send homemade Christmas cookies. I baked the cookies a few days ahead and put them in one of the empty margarine tubs I use to store food. The Sunday before Christmas I hurriedly took the tub out of the refrigerator and wrapped it in bright Christmas paper. Adding a red bow, I thought it made a pretty present. After church we were all hungry, so my husband offered to get lunch. "There's some tuna left over from yesterday," I told him. After searching the refrigerator for a few minutes, he said, "the only container in here is full of Christmas cookies." To my horror I realized I had given my child's Sunday School teacher the leftover tuna!

— *Karen Cogan, TX*

"You can tell that we are in the 1980s. At our Christmas pageant the doll used to represent the Christ child was a Cabbage Patch Preemie."

— *Rev. Eric W. Olsen, NY*

My grandmother was a member of Bethlehem Lutheran Church, Fergus Falls, Minnesota. One Christmas Eve their service ended in time for her to attend the last part of the evening celebration at a nearby Lutheran church. Grandma intended to merely watch from the back of the church. But she startled an usher who offered to seat her when she replied, "Oh, no thank you. I just came from Bethlehem."

— *Karen Svare, MN*

While serving as pastor in Mauldin, SC, I asked the first-year confirmation class, "Who was Martin Luther?" A young teenaged boy replied eagerly, "He was the guy who invented THE LUTHERAN." (magazine)

— *Rodney W. Parrott, SC*

HEY, SEND ME YOUR STORIES!

Chapter 8

Advice Column For Preachers
Dear PK

Dear PK,

Sometimes I feel like I've had enough of preaching, counseling, and altogether dealing with church members' problems. I've got problems of my own, don't people know that?

Signed,
Burned out

Dear Out,

Why don't you quit and get a job on the kill floor of a slaughter house and give yourself a little time to figure out what God had in mind for you. Write me back, I care.

Dear PK,

How do I handle the parents of crying babies when they won't take them out during my sermons?

Signed,
They're driving me crazy!

Dear Crazy,

Make anonymous phone calls to these parents in the middle of the night and cry like a baby. They'll get the message.

Dear PK,

My wife keeps falling asleep during my sermons. What should I do?

> Signed,
> Hurt feelings.

Dear Hurt,

Put her hand in warm water.

Dear PK,

Our P.A. system keeps cutting out during my sermons and the Elders won't get a new one. What should I do?

> Signed,
> End of my rope.

Dear End,

Next Sunday, just whisper the last half of your sermon. The Elders will think they are losing their hearing and will probably get you a new system...or you'll get fired for being a lousy preacher, but that's the chance you take. This has worked many times before though...good luck.

Dear PK,

There are several people that fall asleep during prayers. How should I handle this problem?

> Signed,
> Really perplexed

Dear Really,

Have your congregation stand for all the prayers.

Dear PK,

An old girlfriend has just joined my church. How should I handle this?

> Signed,
> Dumbfounded

Dear Dumb,

Simple, act like you don't remember her.

Dear PK,

Contributions are falling off real bad, how can I turn that around?

> Signed,
> No more money

Dear More,

Tell your congregation that you will be "called home" if you don't raise a specified amount by a certain date. I heard of a preacher from Tulsa doing this.

I don't think it worked for him, but he didn't die either…in case you're worried. Give it a try, what can you lose?

Dear PK,

How do you handle grown-ups who get up in the middle of my sermon to go to the bathroom? Couldn't they go before I started?

Signed,
They're old enough to know better.

Dear Enough,

When these people get up, stop your sermon and ask them to please bring you a glass of water. Shouldn't take over 2-3 times for people to get the message.

Dear PK,

In my adult Sunday school class, there's a man who swears when he gets excited. How do I handle this?

Signed,
Very uncomfortable situation.

Dear Uncomfortable,

Swear right back at him. That'll blow him off his chair. "Oh yeah?" "Yeah!"

Dear PK,

   People who come in late interrupt my sermon and cause a general disruption. How can I put a stop to this?
                        Signed,
                        It's got to stop!

Dear STOP,

   Lock the doors...duh.

Dear PK,

   There are several men who show up Sunday morning and look like they have been out all night partying. How can I get them more involved in church activities?
                        Signed,
                        Mixed up but good men.

Dear Up,

   At the beginning of your next sermon, ask them in front of the entire congregation if they would help out on Saturday nights visiting the elderly and shut-ins.

Dear PK,

   Sometimes I feel like I have to do everything at church myself. What should I do?
                        Signed,
                        Not appreciated enough.

Dear NOT,
When it's time to preach your sermon next Sunday, just sit there... that'll get their attention.

Dear PK,
Church members call me at home with church business on Mondays, which is my only day off. How can I get them to stop?
> Signed,
> Tired of it.

Dear Tired,
Tell them to meet you at your office in 20 minutes and then don't show up.

Dear PK,
I have a hard time getting people to teach kids' Sunday School classes. What would you do?
> Signed,
> Out of gas.

Dear Gas,
Announce that if teachers aren't found, children's Sunday School classes will be held on a rotational basis in members' houses starting next month. That should do it.

Dear PK,

I can't seem to make ends meet on a preacher's salary, what would you do?

Signed,
Broke

Dear Bro.,

Put on dark sun glasses, act blind and sell pencils on the street corner. I'm sure that will help. God bless, let me know how you do. I care.

Dear PK,

I have a hard time getting the congregation's attention at the beginnings of my sermons. Any advice?

Signed,
About to give up.

Dear Give,

Read them a few pages from this book.

Dear PK,

I run into parishioners everywhere I go. I need some time to myself. What'll I do?

Signed,
In need of privacy.

Dear Need,

Wear Groucho glasses, they'll never know it's you.

Dear PK,

People complain that I'm boring and my sermons are too long. Several of them even fake yawns without covering their mouths.

Signed,
I'm going to walk out.

Dear Out,

...I'm sorry, what were you saying?

Dear PK,

My secretary winked at me during my last sermon. How do I handle this?

Signed,
A little confused.

Dear confused,

Ask your wife, I'm sure she'll know what to do.

Dear PK,

There are two young couples in my church who act like they are courting during services instead of worshiping. How shall I handle this?

Signed,
Wrong place.

Dear Wrong,

Throw BB's at them.

Dear PK,

There's a guy in my church who always tells "preacher" jokes. I don't like it.

> Signed,
> No more butt of jokes.

Dear Butt,

Lighten up. Any joke he tells about preachers, just tell the same joke in your next sermon but substitute his occupation in the character. He'll love it, I promise.

Dear PK,

Sometimes the associate pastor only preaches 15 minute sermons. What's his problem?

> Signed,
> Feel cheated.

Dear Cheat,

Who cares what his problem is.

Dear PK,

When there's a blizzard, my elders call off church. What can I do?

> Signed,
> Need to worship.

Dear Need,

Put yoooooour HAND on the radio!

Dear PK,

Sometimes I forget to set my alarm clock and end up sleeping through church. I'm sorry, I don't mean to.
Signed,
Snoozer

Dear Snooze,

Don't worry about it. A lot of people sleep through church...and they're even there.

Dear PK,

I'm the only one at church who doesn't have a job to do.
Signed,
Nobody cares.

Dear Nobody,

So, what's the problem?

Dear PK,

A grown man keeps breaking wind during church. He should know better, what should I do?
Signed,
I've had it.

Dear Had,

Go buy a good bottle of wine, drink it Saturday night and give the tooter the cork on Sunday morning.

Dear PK,

We have a very unruly toddler in our church that disrupts services. What can we do?

Signed,

Can't stand it much longer.

Dear Longer,

Have a designated person sit a couple of rows behind this youngster and everytime the brat misbehaves, shoot him with a power squirt gun. (From your church supply house.) We MUST teach children how to act in church!

Dear PK,

I have a hard time finding a parking spot at church. It makes me so mad I don't even want to go. Any suggestions?

Signed

Running low on gas.

Dear Low,

Don't go. If your church is that packed, nobody will miss you anyway.

Dear PK,

Church is a drag. I should start my own religion.

Signed,

Pooped Out

Dear Pooped,
Go ahead and do it. I'm sure you'll get plenty of support from your present congregation.

Dear PK,
Our church secretary makes numerous mistakes in every Sunday's bulletin. How can I get her to be more careful?
> Signed,
> Tired of it.

Dear Tired,
Don't do anything. Send me the typos if they are funny and tell her to keep up the good work.

Dear PK,
We have an associate pastor who preaches 1 1/2 hour sermons. He's great, you don't even notice the time. When can he speak at your church?
> Signed,
> Feel lucky to have him.

Dear Lucky,
When Hell freezes over.

Dear PK,

We have a song director who always pitches the songs wrong. How can I get rid of him?

> Signed,
> My ears hurt.

Dear Ears,

Sing a different song than he's leading, he'll catch on.

Dear PK,

I'm bored.

> Signed,
> Need a hobby.

Dear Hob,

Start a Dear P column.

Dear PK,

There's one man that comes to church who has terrible body odor. Numerous people have had talks with him, but it doesn't seem to do any good. What in the world should we do?

> Signed,
> He really stinks.

Dear Stink,

Write him a letter and say that new members are welcome and anyone joining our church in the next two weeks will be given free rides to church and free dinners following Sunday services.

Sign it with another church's name. (This is probably how he came to be a member of your church anyway.)

Send your problems to:
Dear PK
P.O. Box 552
York, Nebr. 68467

Chapter 9

Associated Hymns

The chiropractor's hymn—*STAND UP, STAND UP.*

The electrician's hymn—*SEND THE LIGHT.*

The poor person's hymn—*I CARE NOT FOR RICHES.*

The rainmaker's hymn—*SHOWERS OF BLESS-ING.*

The surgical patient's hymn—*I LONG TO BE PERFECTLY WHOLE.*

The day you find out you're pregnant hymn—*O HAPPY DAY.*

The day you find out you're NOT pregnant hymn—*O HAPPY DAY.*

The Mountain Home Builder's Association hymn—*MY HOUSE IS BUILT UPON A ROCK.*

My kid's getting even with me hymn—*O THEY TELL ME OF A HOME.*

The ranger station hymn—*ON A HILL FAR AWAY.*

The physical therapist hymn—*ONE STEP AT A TIME.*

The divorced person's hymn—*OUT OF MY BONDAGE.*

The WIDE LOAD hymn—*PASS ME NOT.*

The rescuer's hymn—*SEEKING THE LOST.*

The fisherman's hymn—*SHALL WE GATHER AT THE RIVER.*

The last payment hymn—*SINCE I CAN READ MY TITLE CLEAR.*

The seamstress hymn—*SOWING IN THE MORNING.*

The dater's hymn—*THE NIGHT IS FAST PASSING.*

The thirsty person's hymn—*THERE IS A FOUNTAIN.*

The slingshot hymn—*THERE IS A ROCK.*

The telephone repairman's hymn—*THERE'S A CALL COMES RINGING.*

The dieter's hymn—*THOU, MY EVER LASTING PORTION.*

The chain gang hymn—*GO LABOR ON.*

The hiker's hymn—*WALKING IN THE SUNLIGHT.*

The car accident hymn—*WE SAW THEE NOT.*

The lawyer's hymn—*WHEN ALL MY LABORS AND TRIALS ARE O'ER.*

The street crossing guard hymn—*WHY DO YOU WAIT?*

The prisoner's hymn—*WOULD YOU BE FREE.*

The home builder's hymn—*A MIGHTY FORTRESS.*

The parade master's hymn—*FLING OUT THE BANNER.*

The weatherman's hymn—*FROM EVERY STORMY WIND THAT BLOWS.*

The Darning Association's hymn—*HOLY, HOLY, HOLY.*

The Girdle Association hymn—*HOW FIRM A FOUNDATION.*

The caterer's hymn—*ALL THINGS ARE READY, COME TO THE FEAST.*

The salesman's hymn—*ALMOST PERSUADED.*

The insurance man's hymn—*BLESSED ASSURANCE.*

The cowboy's hymn—*DAY IS DYING IN THE WEST.*

The accountant's hymn—*EARTH HOLDS NO TREASURES.*

The traveler's hymn—*FAR AND NEAR.*

The scuba diver's hymn—*FAR AWAY IN THE DEPTHS.*

The whisperer's hymn—*HARK! THE GENTLE VOICE.*

The whining spouse hymn—*HAVE THINE OWN WAY.*

The wagon master's hymn—*HE LEADETH ME.*

The hearing aid salesman's hymn—*HEAR THE SWEET VOICE.*

The lost traveler's hymn—*HERE WE ARE BUT STRAYING PILGRIMS.*

The oxen hymn—*HIS YOKE IS EASY.*

The new kid in class hymn—*I AM A STRANGER HERE.*

The rookie hang glider's hymn—*I AM DWELLING ON THE MOUNTAIN.*

The Vegetable Grower's Association hymn—*I COME TO THE GARDEN ALONE.*

The explorer's hymn—*I HAVE HEARD OF A LAND.*

The watch repairman's hymn—*I NEED THEE EVERY HOUR.*

The Job Service hymn—*I WANT TO BE A WORKER.*

The ironing lady's hymn—*I'M PRESSING ON.*

The distiller's hymn—*I REACHED THE LAND OF CORN AND WINE.*

The lost dog hymn—*I'VE WANDERED FAR.*

The half time Alaska hymn—*IN THE LAND OF FADELESS DAY.*

The birthday hymn—*IS IT FOR ME?*

The night watchman's hymn—*IT MAY BE AT MORN.*

The nervous groom's hymn—*JUST A FEW MORE DAYS.*

The perfect person's hymn—*JUST AS I AM.*

The drunkard's hymn—*LEAD ME GENTLY HOME.*

The psychiatrist hymn—*LET US WITH A GLAD-SOME MIND.*

The pie maker's hymn—*PEACE, PERFECT PEACE.*

The Gold Collector's Association hymn—*PURER YET AND PURER.*

The Rock Collector's Association hymn—*ROCK OF AGES.*

The dynamite specialist hymn—*SAFELY THROUGH ANOTHER WEEK.*

The race car hymn—*SPEED AWAY.*

The payment book hymn—*WE GIVE THEE BUT THINE OWN.*

The escaped convict's hymn—*FLEE AS A BIRD.*

The coal miner's hymn—*SOMEWHERE THE SUN IS SHINING.*

Chapter 10

Sunday Mornin' Shame

Sing to the chorus of
THROW OUT THE LIFELINE
or read as a poem.

— *Ken Alley*

1st verse
No time for Jesus
No time for Jesus
Sunday mornin' shame.

I've told you before
there's just one to adore
and he doesn't have your
name.

Look in the mirror
and check if God's nearer
or see why your life is a
pain.

No time for Jesus
No time for Jesus
Sunday mornin' shame.

2nd verse
Pray on the golf course
Pray on the golf course
Sunday mornin' shame.

You won't go to heaven
By bogeying seven
and taking his name in
vain.

But forsaking assembly
Means one thing simply,
that God might not
know your name.

Pray on the golf course
Pray on the golf course
Sunday mornin' shame.

3rd verse

Sleeping in on Sunday
Sleeping in on Sunday
Sunday mornin' shame.

When you're out of
excuses
with no more rebukeses
and no one will think
you sane.

It doesn't bother
that things get hotter
when you singe your butt
on the flames.

Sleeping in on Sunday
Sleeping in on Sunday
Sunday mornin' shame.

4th verse

Being late for worship
Being late for worship
Sunday mornin' shame.

There's nothing sadder
When it doesn't matter
and there's no one else
to blame.

Nothin' will be sweeter
Than talking to St. Peter
When the end is here to
stay.

Being late for worship
Being late for worship
Sunday mornin' shame.

5th verse (sing with gusto)

Always move ova
Because of Jehovah
Give him the right of
way.

Don't wait for Easter
to pray for your keester
'cause no one can run
away.

If you're a geezer
and next for the freezer
Don't gamble your life
today.

There's no way of
knowin'
if you're comin' or goin'
Sunday mornin' shame.

Conclusion
(Backward)

"Dear PK" was a brainstorm that hit me early one morning as I was sitting in my easy chair drinking coffee. I was thinking of the Dear Abby column where there was always answers for problems.

I made up questions that preachers and parishioners would ask and then formulated smart alec answers. I got the giggles so hard that little squeaks came out of my mouth. My wife heard me and jumped out of bed because she thought I was having a heart attack. An hour later in the shower, it hit me again and I started squeaking again. You can only imagine these sounds coming from a bathroom.

The idea for Associated Hymns came from a Lutheran magazine where a fellow did a similar thing. I tried and tried to locate him so I could get his permission to put his "Occupational Airs" in my book, but I couldn't find him. The next best thing was to swipe one of my own church hymnals and write my own. So, I did. A lot of laughs came from developing this part of ONCE UPON A PEW.

I guess this book has been an outlet for me. Humorous situations have always been a kick, but deep down I also feel this book might humanize church somewhat. Many people have quit going to church not because of a problem with God, but because of conflicts with other members. Maybe if they read this book, it will remind them that although individual personalities make up a congregation, God still wants their cans at church.

I hope you have enjoyed reading this book as much as I have had putting it together. Maybe I'll get a better parking stall in heaven for my endeavor.

Please send me your "True Bloopers" for future books about church, doctor/hospital visits, farmlife, classrooms, jobs, or life in general. Your name will be credited unless you wish to remain anonymous. Thanks a bunch!

I will be writing these books forever, so don't think you are "too late" to submit anything.

Send all submissions to:

Bloopers
P.O. Box 552
York, Nebraska 68467

MAKE SOMEONE SMILE.

GOD BLESS

Copies of this book can be obtained at your favorite bookstore or by sending $10.95 (plus $3 s&h & .75 for each additional book) to PEW, P.O. Box 552, York, Nebraska 68467.

Overseas add additional $3 per book.

COMING SOON!
More true humor.

LIFE'S A GAS (if you look close.)

ALSO

PREACHERS, CHURCH AND OTHER HEAVENLY THINGS.
Great humorous anecdotes!

All media are welcomed to use individual excerpts from these books without seeking permission as long as credit is given to the book.